Girls

V

K

KITTY DIMBLEBY

Daffodil Girls

*Stories of love, loss and friendship from the
women behind our heroes*

One hundred per cent of the author's royalties for the hardback edition of this book, less the author's advance, have been donated to Help for Heroes Trading Limited, which gift aids all its taxable profits to Help for Heroes (Registered Charity Number 1120920).

2 4 6 8 10 9 7 5 3 1

First published in 2011 by Virgin Books, an imprint of Ebury Publishing

A Random House Group Company

This edition published in 2012 by Virgin Books

www.randomhouse.co.uk

Addresses for companies within The Random House Group Limited can be

A CIP   British Library

The Ran   rdship Council
(FSC®),   ion. Our books
carrying   SC is the only
fore   onmental
orga   ment policy
                                                                nent

FSC
www.fsc.org   FSC® C016897

responsible sources

ISBN: 9780753539651

Printed and bound by CPI Group (UK) Ltd, Croydon, CR0 4YY

To buy books by your favourite authors and register for offers, visit:
www.randomhouse.co.uk

This book is dedicated to the families of the members of our armed forces, past, present and future.
And to Annabel, the newest Daffodil bud on the patch.

CONTENTS

FOREWORD

While the lives of our soldiers have changed dramatically over the years – the conflict zones they fight in, the enemies they face and the experience of war itself – not much has changed in the life of an army wife. The time drags when they are away – six months feels like six years, the anxiety is crippling, it is terribly lonely and only those who have lived it can really understand what you are going through. I know because I've been there; first back in 1981 when my fiancé was on an operational tour of Northern Ireland and then in 2009, when my son was deployed to Helmand in Afghanistan. You have to be as brave, albeit in a different way, as the soldier you love, keeping the life they have left behind running in their absence, while also living with terrible fear – not of a bullet or a mortar, but a knock on the door bringing the news you dread.

Daffodil Girls is the story of the countless unsung heroines of army life: the women who have to sit and wait for their loved ones to return from increasingly dangerous operational tours, all the time desperately trying to keep their darkest thoughts at bay - what if the soldier they love comes back changed, injured or, unbearably, doesn't come back at all?

In the summer of 2007 my husband Bryn and I met some of those wounded, and their families, and decided we had to do something – Help for Heroes was born. The aim was to provide direct practical support to those injured in the service of our country, and therefore also their families. The message of the charity would be strictly non-political and non-critical, giving people a chance to 'do their bit' to show these extraordinary men and women that they are cared about by us, the British public.

Three and a half years on and the response has been phenomenal. The money donated to Help for Heroes (a total of £110m at time of going to print) is used in a huge variety of ways. The first major undertaking was the £8m state-of-the-art gym and swimming pool complex at DMRC (Defence Medical Rehabilitation Centre) Headley Court, which opened in June 2010. The next big project will be the Personnel Recovery Centres planned for Edinburgh, Colchester, Catterick, Tidworth and Plymouth. The centres will provide individually tailored care for the wounded, teach them new skills and provide access to comprehensive support, ranging from medical and psychological care, to financial and employment assistance. The intention is to create a 'one-stop welfare shop' so army personnel can leave the centres fully prepared to tackle the next stage of their lives, knowing exactly where to go for help if they have problems.

In an initiative close to my heart, because it enables us to directly support the loved ones as well as the serving personnel, in 2010 Help for Heroes launched the Quick Reaction Fund, a £6m fund that provides financial help to wounded individuals and their relatives within 72 hours of receiving a request. The funds, administered by the Services' own charities, will ensure that individuals and their families can access Help for Heroes aid when it is needed most. For example, if a wounded serviceman needs his home upgraded to enable him to live there and there were no other funds available, the Quick Reaction Fund would pay for the upgrade. Similarly, if a relative has run into financial difficulty as a result of staying at their loved one's bedside, the Fund can be used to help.

Kitty Dimbleby has been involved with Help for Heroes from day one. When her husband was in Iraq in 2007, she wrote one of the first articles about the new charity and, since becoming an army wife, Kitty has worked full-time as a vital part of our media team.

As the wife of a soldier, Kitty has struggled with the same sense of separation and anxiety that befalls all army wives. Her unique and very personal insight into the lives of the women married to members of 2 Royal Welsh – a few of whom, I am proud to say, also work with us at Help for Heroes - has produced a story that often had me reaching for the Kleenex, and which reinforces what a tough job it is to be left behind. She has given these women a voice and reminded us that behind every single member of our armed forces fighting on the front line are the wives, girlfriends, mothers and daughters keeping the modern-day home fires burning. These are the heroines behind our heroes.

Emma Parry OBE, co-founder of Help for Heroes

INTRODUCTION

My knowledge of the military was pretty limited back in 2005. To be honest, I gave the army little thought, only pausing occasionally at the obituary images in the newspapers of uniformed men and women. Theirs was a world that I knew little about, and one which I believed had no real relevance to my life. Amazing how things change. At the end of that year, when I was twenty-five, I met and fell in love with an army officer, and the shadowy idea I'd had of 'a soldier' very quickly became replaced by the flesh-and-blood men with whom I now began to spend time.

Ed comes from a long line of soldiers. When we met, his father and uncle, both colonels in the same regiment, were serving away from home in Kosovo and Turkey. Ed's grandfather was a decorated World War One hero who died from his injuries before Ed was born. Ed's military lineage was as long and impressive as my journalistic one and I was fascinated by the world in which he had grown up: boarding school from the age of eight, living on 'the patch' – the slang name given to the housing estates for married service personnel which surround military garrisons, moving every two years, his father away frequently – sometimes for seven months at a time. It all seemed impossibly hard to me, so I was deeply impressed by the stoic nature of his mother and grandmother – army wives through and through who had kept the home fires burning, first for their husbands and then their sons.

I resolved to be the model army girlfriend – supportive and uncomplaining. But of course at that time I had no idea how hard this would really be. Through Ed I met other women of my generation – army WAGs we jokingly called ourselves – and soon I had a new group of friends, always on the end of an email or the phone, to support one another through the ups and downs of army WAGdom. I met men and women of all military ranks and from differing backgrounds, their partners and their families – and my understanding and admiration for our armed forces grew and grew.

I was still a journalist, however, and could not help but be fascinated by the stories they told, from day-to-day life in a war zone to the difficult wait back at home. Moved and awed in equal measure, I felt these first-hand accounts painted a far more vivid picture of events in Afghanistan and Iraq – and the consequent fall-out at home for families – than anything I had ever read or seen on the news. This was real life; straight from soldiers' mouths and from the point of view of those who love them.

In the summer of 2007, when my soldier boyfriend was sent to Iraq, I experienced for myself the agony endured by the thousands of military families whose loved ones are in a war zone. I do not use the word 'agony' here lightly, for only those who have lived through it can truly understand the constant worry, and sometime crippling fear, felt by those left behind. The result was that I decided to use my journalism to try to convey the sacrifices made not only by the men and women who go to war, but also by those who wait for them at home. I wrote a major feature for the *Mail on Sunday* about the 'e-bluey' letter-writing system, and also about an internet chat room which the families of serving soldiers, airmen and seamen use to support one another. My personal experience I hope, helped to anchor the stories of these brave, ordinary individuals who keep the home fires burning while their loved ones are at war. For I, too, was now receiving letters and phone calls from my boyfriend, each of which painted a vivid picture of life in the conflict zone. Personally, they gave comfort; professionally, they enthralled me and left me wanting to learn more.

So in August 2007, inspired by a story I had seen on the Ministry of Defence website, I flew to Iraq to meet a group of soldiers and write about their work with a local orphanage. It was a dangerous time to be in Basra and I was the last journalist ever to report from Basra Palace while it was under British control, and we were mortared relentlessly. At the same time, however, I witnessed life out there first-hand; the stoical nature of members of our armed forces, and the dignity and gentle humour with which they conduct themselves. Of course the men and women I met talked about their loved ones back home, about the letters and parcels sent, the phone calls, and about how they try to stop their families worrying. Despite being in a war zone it was clear that those left at home helped to shape the stories of the men and women at war, with news from home having the ability to lift or lower the mood of the toughest of soldiers.

In October 2007 I visited Headley Court, the military rehabilitation centre in Surrey, where I met with injured men and women in order to write the first article about Help For Heroes, a then-new charity which has since gone on to become a household name. Every individual I met – some with shocking injuries – talked more of the bravery, love and support of their family than of their own suffering. This cemented for me the idea that it is the army of people waiting at home that enables our armed forces to do their job.

A year later, in 2008, I became engaged to my own soldier and a week later left him behind for Afghanistan. I travelled throughout the country – from Kabul to Kandahar and to Lashkar Gah – until I reached Camp Bastion, the military base in Helmand province, where I spent four days embedded with the Medical Emergency Response Team (MERT). Living, eating and working with the team, which flies day and night across Southern Afghanistan to pick up the injured, was a daunting experience and my respect for these men and women is boundless. At every turn, it seemed, I was confronted with deeply humbling tales of heroism, each told without fuss by people ranging from an eighteen-year-old squaddie to a fifty-two-year-old army surgeon.

Again, it was the stories these people told of home that sparked my imagination. Sitting in a tent with four men while each wrote to their loved ones – well, even the hardest of hearts would have been moved. A captain wrote to his unborn son – asking if he was kicking more and telling him to look after mummy. Apparently he and his wife had agreed this method of letter writing – the realities of his grim life on the front line too much for a pregnant women waiting at home alone. Another captain wrote to his new girlfriend, 'my darling', 'my love' and told me that writing his daily missive – and her response – got him through the week. A sergeant wrote to his five-year-old – each letter large and well shaped so his little boy, learning to read, could copy his words. 'It's hard when you miss the important things,' he stated, simply.

I decided I wanted to tell the stories of those who are left behind, to tell the story of a tour from the point of view of the families waiting at home. Each fighting their own battle, one where you do not win or lose, just survive until your loved one returns to you. There is an army at home – the grandparents, mothers, girlfriends, wives, husbands, boyfriends, children and friends whose love and support enable our military to do the job asked of them under the most terrible of circumstances. It is the story of those left behind that has to be told and which will, I hope, provide a unique and valuable insight into modern-day warfare and the courage of the most ordinary of people.

The 2nd Battalion Royal Welsh is an armoured infantry battalion based at Tidworth in Wiltshire, the same garrison town as my husband's regiment, the King's Royal Hussars.

The Royal Welsh was formed on St David's Day 2006 from two historic line infantry regiments: the 1st Battalion Royal Welch Fusiliers and The 1st Battalion The Royal Regiment of Wales. Since the amalgamation, 2 R Welsh has completed one tour of Iraq and sent companies of 150 men on three tours of Afghanistan (the most recent of which will still not be completed at the time of this book going to print). In this time, six 2 R Welsh soldiers have lost their lives. The battalion has endured one of the most continued periods of fighting of any regiment in the British Army, and as such, was the perfect battalion to follow for this project. I met Amanda and Kirsty, two of the Daffodil Girls – the nickname I have given the women who agreed to be interviewed for this book – at Help for Heroes where they both work and Amanda, a senior Daffodil Girl with huge standing within the battalion wives and soldiers' community, liked my idea for this book and offered to help. Within days I had a meeting with the commanding officer and a number of wives willing to talk to me. The project, which I had been trying to get off the ground for months, was kick-started within hours by Amanda, proving, undoubtedly, the power of the wives' club.

I spent much of the summer and autumn of 2010 with the wives of 2 Royal Welsh. Some husbands were away in Afghanistan, others had recently returned; each of the women had unique and remarkable stories to tell. In this book, I have tried to pull together their tales to create the definitive story of an army tour from the wives' perspective: the preparation, the tour, and the homecoming. The material is drawn from the experiences of recent and current tours in Afghanistan and Iraq. I have endeavoured to be as current as possible and, at the time of going to print, two of the Daffodil Girls' husbands, Lee and Ben, are still away, fighting on the front line in Afghanistan.

I must also quantify that I am very aware that the army is only one-third of our wonderful armed forces and that there are countless RAF and British Navy families going through the pain of separation from their loved ones. This book is based on what I know, about being married to a soldier and living in an army community. I also know that there are many brave women who go to war leaving husbands and boyfriends at home to worry, that of course there are also fathers who have a child sent to a war zone, and supportive girlfriends who keep the home fire burning away from the regimental family. This book, however, is about the world I inhabit in Tidworth and the wives' community, the people who are my neighbours and my friends.

INTRODUCING THE DAFFODIL GIRLS

I have chosen to only use first names throughout the book for continuity – most of the women and their husbands were happy to be identified in full but, because there are a few examples where sensitivities meant I would only be referring to the individual by their first name, I decided to take this approach across the whole book.

Amanda, 38, wife of Captain Lee, 41;
two daughters, Megan, 17, and Bethan, 15.

Clare, 32, former soldier, married to the welfare officer, Mo;
two children, Kimberley, seven months, and Ryan, four.

Dereynn, 46, married to Sergeant Taff, 44;
two children, Sian, 24, (now married to her own soldier, Alex, and has a daughter, Bailey-Mae aged six months), and Gav, 19.

Donna, 21, married to Private Craig, 20;
one son, Bradley, aged three.

Elaine, 30, married to Corporal Pete, 33;
three children, Aaron, 13, Bethany, 11, and Lewis,
aged seven.

Julie, 38, married to Captain Dai, 41;
two children, Macaulay, 15, and Morgan, 12.

Kaz, 43, married to Lance Corporal Brian, 28;
one daughter, Megan, 18.

Kirsty, 24, married to Lieutenant Benedict (Ben for short), 25.

Mandy, 37, married to Sergeant Major Ian, 38;
two children, Cerys, 13, and Shaun, 11.

Rhiannon, 35, married to Major Huw, 36.

Sarah, 44, mother of Private James, 21.

Simone, 37, married to Sergeant Major Mark, 39;
two children, Dale, 19, and Brad, 15.

UNDERSTANDING ARMY RANKS

SOLDIERS' RANKS
Private
Lance Corporal
Corporal
Sergeant
Colour Sergeant
Warrant Officer class 2 (Sergeant Major)
Warrant Officer class 1 (Regimental Sergeant Major RSM)

OFFICERS' RANKS
2nd Lieutenant
Lieutenant
Captain (direct entry or late entry; direct entry meaning someone who has joined the army as an officer, a 2nd Lieutenant, straight from Sandhurst; late entry, someone who has worked their way up through the ranks, becoming

a captain after being a WO1)
Major
Lieutenant Colonel
Colonel
Brigadier
Major General
Lieutenant General
General.

PART ONE

PRE-TOUR

PROLOGUE

'Knowing He's Going To Go'

It was 3.30am and still dark when the alarm went off but Kirsty and Ben were already wide-awake. Sitting up in bed, Kirsty watched while her husband of just eight months collected together the last of his belongings and dressed in his combat uniform. The couple were silent – there was too much to be said to even try and start at this late juncture.

Kirsty had been crying sporadically throughout the night. Despite the best intentions to dress up for their goodbye, she had only the energy to pull on some tracksuit bottoms and a T-shirt, really the most comfortable things to wear over her growing six-month baby bump. Her eyes were so red and sore that she didn't even bother with her contact lenses and left her hair messed up from the pillow.

This was to be the couple's first experience of a tour, with Second Lieutenant Benedict not long out of Sandhurst. The couple had married just days before they moved to the patch in Tidworth when Benedict officially joined the battalion. Kirsty had been dreading this separation – not least because the time he would be away would coincide with the arrival of their first child. Mandy had been married to a soldier for fourteen years, but his latest tour, starting just two days before their wedding anniversary, was definitely the hardest goodbye. Her eldest child, their daughter Cerys, thirteen, wanted to go with her mum to drop off her dad in camp but Shaun, their son, decided to say his goodbyes in the kitchen at home. Just ten years old at the time, he knew he now had to be the man of the house, so grabbing a bowl of cereal he gave his dad a manly pat on the back, saying 'See you soon' before heading up to his room to play on his Playstation.

Donna tried to be really brave when she said goodbye to Craig. She wanted to show her husband how strong she could be so that, during the course of their six-month separation, his mind would be on his job, not worrying about the little family he had left behind. Married for less than a year, they both knew this time was going to be tougher for Donna than the time before. Then, when Private Craig had gone to Iraq, the couple were engaged but Donna was living in Catterick near her family, friends and familiar life.

Now, living on the patch in Tidworth, Donna was far from the supportive network she had enjoyed the previous tour. She knew the girls on the patch would be there for her but she was all too aware that many would be going home to their families. Donna had decided to stay put, not wanting to uproot their three-year-old son any more than necessary – even if that did mean she was in for a lonely six months.

When Amanda had found out a few months previously that her husband Lee was going away for his ninth tour of duty, she had sat at the kitchen table during supper and sobbed. 'It sounds dramatic,' she says, 'but I felt as if we'd been dropped a bombshell – I really didn't want him to go.' But the night before Lee left there were no tears; the family watched TV and their eldest daughter Megan, seventeen, fell asleep on the sofa. When she came to say goodnight to her dad she was half-asleep – too dopey to get upset, it was almost like any other bedtime. But that was the last time she would see her dad before he left – the whole family had decided that it was easier for all involved if Lee slipped away in the morning without waking the girls.

Their younger daughter, fifteen-year-old Bethan, stayed up with her parents until past midnight. When Lee left the room for a moment Bethan took the chance to confess to her mum that she couldn't bear to say goodbye, that she was scared, scared of breaking down in front of her dad, scared about where he was going. Father and daughter hugged goodbye for a long time that night. It was a sleepless one for the couple and their youngest child.

In the run-up to her husband leaving, Elaine couldn't help but count down the days, then the hours, then the minutes. Corporal Pete was collected from the terraced army quarter at around four o'clock. The couple had got up together, then Elaine busied herself making a cup of tea while Pete gathered the last of his things.

Elaine remembers feeling just horrible, 'Knowing he's going to go . . . and he might not come back. I think every-one feels the same'. I went to wave him off on the doorstep, and my neighbour Louise was stood on her doorstep waving her husband off as well. We couldn't help but smile when we realised we were both stood there in the same pyjamas – three-quarter pink ones with hearts on, from the local Tesco.'

Kirsty and Benedict were still unable to talk as they drove into camp. They played the radio to disguise the oppressive silence between them. Playing was the Europop hit *We No Speak Americano*. Kirsty remembers thinking how inappropriate it was for the mood of the journey and yet, days later, she was unable to get the annoyingly catchy song out of her mind.

In camp, they parked up by the parade ground, in a quiet spot, for their goodbye. Kirsty waited in the car while Benedict unloaded his kit and took his bags to the army vehicles waiting over the road. When he returned after the third trip, he got back into the car and they shared a hug.

'I didn't want to let go,' says Kirsty. 'The car handbrake was digging into my bump and it was really uncomfortable but I ignored it. Finally we both got out of the car to swap seats and stood hugging by the driver's door.

'I couldn't really say anything because the worst thoughts were going through my head and I didn't want my parting words to be something horrible and negative. The night before I wasn't strong enough and I already felt guilty; I kept saying stupid things, like, "What if this is the last time I see you?" He hates that and I shouldn't say it. But, as always, he was so good about it and even when he was hugging me, saying goodbye, he was being practical and loving – worrying whether or not I knew my way out of camp because the one-way route had changed since I had last driven it. I loved how concerned he was, but also it really brought home how alone I would now be.'

For Mandy and Cerys, dropping Company Sergeant Major Ian at camp was far more emotional than the farewell shared between father and son. Cerys climbed out of the car with her dad to say goodbye while mum Mandy hung back – letting her daughter have a moment alone.

Then it was Mandy's turn. 'We stood by the car and Ian laughed and called me a silly sod when I started to get emotional. We told one another we loved one another and that we would see each other soon. Then he walked off and left us there. His last words to me before he walked away – dressed in his desert combat with his bags slung over his shoulder were "The more you cry, the less you pee" – it wasn't very romantic, but that's what he always says to me. It makes me laugh no matter how much I am crying.'

When the time came, Benedict told Kirsty he had to leave. 'I wanted to cling to him but that would have been too hard, for both of us. I kept telling him to be safe and he promised me he would be. Watching him walk away was the hardest thing I have ever had to do. I was crying too much to drive off immediately so I stayed in the car, out of sight, until I felt calm enough to leave.'

Amanda had hoped that saying goodbye to Lee would be slightly easier this time; he wasn't wearing uniform, having taken it into camp the day before. 'I'd hoped it would feel less like a tour, that I would be able to temporarily fool myself that he was just popping out, but of course that wasn't the case.

'I watched the bus go and I sobbed. It feels wrong to compare it to bereavement – because I've lost people close to me – but it is suffocating. You struggle to breathe when they first leave and it's panic, because you just want them back, but there's nothing you can do about it.'

Cerys and Mandy drove back home both half-crying and half-laughing at one another for being so soft. Five minutes after they got back, Ian texted to tell Mandy to go look on their bed, where he'd left her a gift and a card. Even though they'd agreed to do nothing for their anniversary both had ignored that, Mandy putting a card in Ian's bag for him to find when he got to Afghanistan. But, she hadn't been expecting anything from him.

The gift was a glass paperweight with a red heart, with a little note saying, 'Please look after my heart while I'm away. We'll celebrate our next wedding anniversary in more style.' Ian had also left Cerys a note which read, 'Look after your brother, and behave. Help your mother out with the housework. Know I always love you, and I'll ring you as soon as I can.' 'So she starting crying,' Mandy remembers, 'and I was already crying . . .'

There was still one final message to come from Ian before he left: a text to Mandy as he was about to board his plane at RAF Brize Norton. 'Love you,' he wrote, 'and speak to you soon.' 'That was it,' Mandy remembers thinking. 'He was gone.'

*

There was a final goodbye, too, for one of the other Daffodil Girls. The following day Donna was adjusting to the idea that her husband had left when, with no warning, he appeared at the front door. En route from the sitting room to the kitchen, Donna was stopped in her tracks by the sight of Craig, dressed in his desert combats, filling the small hallway of their army quarter. Standing an imposing six foot three inches, Craig filled most rooms in the house – but his vivacious personality was as much to blame for this as his bulk.

Donna felt a myriad emotions: surprise at seeing him, inexplicably shy and awkward – and slightly frustrated that they would have to go through their goodbye all over again. 'What you doing back?' she asked. Craig explained that his departure from camp had been delayed, so he and a mate had decided to sneak off for one last kiss goodbye with their wives.

'This is it this time,' he told her before lifting her on to one of the kitchen chairs to give her a kiss and a cuddle. At five foot four, Donna was just under a foot shorter than her husband so this was the only way for them to say goodbye eye-to-eye. 'I was trying not to show emotion,' Donna recalls, 'because I didn't want him to think I was at home alone, all upset. If they're focusing too much on home that could mean they are distracted and in a war zone that could get them killed. Craig said, "I'm going to miss you. Make sure you look after Bradley." I can't remember the last words we said, but it was probably, "Keep safe". I used to say that a lot.'

Donna remembers Craig lifting her down off the chair. 'He grabbed me because I'm so short. We were kissing and when he let go of me on the floor he let go of me from the kiss as well. He said – in between kisses – he had to go now and that was it. I watched him get in the car and waved – but I could only wave so much because the bushes were in the way. And I thought he's gone – he's gone for real this time.'

CHAPTER 1

'I Never Set Out To Marry A Soldier'

The Daffodil Girls is a tale that begins with a goodbye. Because for an army wife, watching your loved one leave to spend many months away is a moment that goes with the territory. It is a rite of passage that the partners of every rank and regiment have to go through, that the wives of 2 Royal Welsh are all too familiar with, and one that I know myself. As well as being a writer, I too am an army wife. Or maybe I should say, that as well as being an army wife, I am also a writer. That might sound a strange way to put it, but being married to a soldier is different to saying 'I do' to a doctor, a tradesman or a banker: it is a way of life that defines who you are. That's why I wanted to write this book – to show through the experiences of one battalion's wives what being an army wife is all about.

Like many of the Daffodil Girls, I never set out to marry a soldier. I met Ed for the first time a week before he left for

Iraq, when he held a joint leaving party with a good friend of mine from university. I was seeing someone at the time – as was Ed – but six months later, post-tour, our mutual friend brought Ed to a Halloween party my flatmate and I were hosting. I was impressed by the effort he had gone to over his costume – a native American Indian-turned-zombie, complete with white face paint and convincing blood. He joined our group of friends easily and confidently. When the time came for the group to leave my tiny two-bedroom flat and move on to a club down the road, I called him over, saying, 'You look like you have a loud voice, can you get this lot to leave?' Leave they did, and that night he and I kissed and danced and talked (in that order).

The next day I emailed a girlfriend, telling her about him and ending my message with the now-immortal line, 'There is a real chemistry but he's in the army, so it is just going to be a fling.' Attracted though I was by Ed's confidence, manners and cavalry-officer charm, I was never going to fall for an army boy – much less marry one. His was a world that I did not understand, nor had I any desire to do so.

All who knew me universally mocked the idea of me becoming an army wife. It seemed a strange idea to me, too, though like most people on Civvy Street, my feelings were based on that inconsistent mix of not really knowing what being an army wife meant, while at the same time being sure that whatever it was, it wasn't really for me. But as my relationship with Ed became more serious, so the possibility of my marrying a soldier became increasingly likely. It was time to put my preconceptions aside and find the answer to the question I'd so far been avoiding. What does it really mean to be an army wife?

The first time the Daffodil Girls met their future husbands, the fact that they were talking to a soldier was secondary to how the men looked, what they said, and that sparkle in their eye. Listening to each of them tell, with warmth and humour, their stories of how they got together, it's easy to forget what these women's husbands do for a day job – for this moment at least, the Daffodil Girls are like any other group of girlfriends, reminiscing about the day they fell in love.

It had been just another night at her local nightclub in Catterick for Donna, until she caught sight of Craig. She had been standing in the DJ booth, chatting to a friend, when she saw him: tall, smiling and handsome, and wearing a Welsh rugby top. Donna can't remember exactly what is was about him that caught her eye, but he immediately stood out from the group of mates he was dancing with. Donna didn't usually do this sort of thing, but she found herself pushing through the throng of dancing revellers in order to speak to him.

When she finally got over to where he was dancing, the music was so loud that Donna had to shout to make herself heard. Not only that, but she had to stand on tiptoe to reach his ear.

'Are you Welsh?' she asked.

'Yes,' Craig shouted back.

The couple starting talking, or at least tried to start talking over the music before having a dance. Craig, as he had now introduced himself, took Donna to the bar where he bought her a drink. They sat down in a corner where they started to get to know one another properly. They got on well immediately, but when she found out he was a soldier, Donna's instant reaction was that this was unlikely to go any further. Living in a garrison town, Donna was used to soldiers and the fact that they rarely called when they said they would do so. So even though Craig promised to call, and they shared a kiss that night, Donna said goodbye not expecting to hear from him again.

For Julie, her relationship with Dai was almost over before it had begun. It was a Friday night and she had got dressed up to the nines for their first date: long blonde hair piled up on her head, the smallest of miniskirts grazing her thighs, a crop top and knee-high boots. If she was being honest, she hadn't been completely sure about Dai when she had first met him through a friend, but after a year of him visiting her home village in Wales, she had slowly got to know him. So when he asked her out on a date, she said yes. But with no sign of him as first the minutes and then the hours started to tick by, she was beginning to regret accepting.

It wasn't until the next day that Dai called, full of apologies. His explanation for standing her up was perhaps not the strongest of excuses – a drink or two with some mates had turned into a bit of a session and he had fallen asleep. Even so, there was something about him that persuaded Julie to give him a second chance. She got dressed up again, but once more Dai failed to show up. By this point, Julie was livid but, even so, something still told her not to give up – on the Sunday he did show up and, taking her to the local pub, introduced her to most of his family. 'It was a bit of a shock,' says Julie, 'but I got to know him and,' she remembers fondly, 'that was it.'

Liverpudlian Dereynn was on holiday in Penbryn Sands when she met her future husband, Taff. Not only was he younger than her (she was twenty, he eighteen), his case wasn't helped by one of the corniest chat-up lines to open with, when he asked, 'Do you come here often?' There was something about his smile, though, that Dereynn couldn't help but like, and even though she didn't expect to find anything in common with a boy from the valleys, something clicked. When it was time for the holiday to end, the pair agreed to stay in touch.

Amanda, meanwhile, had long admired her school friend's elder brother, Lee. Lee, too, had noticed the pretty blonde friend of his little sister, but decided that at sixteen, she was too young for him. Two years later, however, and with Amanda now eighteen, Lee showed up at her house. Now twenty-one and a soldier, Lee was on Easter leave when he decided to pluck up the courage to ask her out for a drink. Amanda said yes. Things went well and walking her home that night, Lee asked if he could take her out again, properly, the following evening. Lee took her to watch a show in the local pub – appropriately enough, given his battalion, this first 'proper' date was on St David's Day.

Amanda was smitten and so, it seemed, was Lee: he asked to see her again the following day. That evening, Amanda's mum was walking her to the bus stop when a breathless and apologetic Lee ran past them – in the wrong direction. He was running late, he explained and would meet her there as soon as he could. Amanda's response was one of annoyance but as the pair watched Lee disappear, her mum knew better.

'You're going to marry him,' she said.

'Don't be daft,' retorted Amanda.

Her mum, though, was certain. 'I'm telling you now – you're going to marry him.'

For Kirsty, the moment when she knew things were about to change was when Benedict suggested they sneak away from their friends in the club, and go for a walk along the seafront. Kirsty had first met Ben a couple of years earlier when they both had summer jobs at a local theme park, and they had been good friends ever since. She had liked him for ages, and thought that he felt the same about her, but girlfriends, boyfriends and bad timing had always conspired to keep them apart. Now, however, both were single, and working and living in the same area: Kirsty as a trainee reporter on the local paper, Ben at a school while he waited for term to begin on his officer cadet course at Sandhurst.

It was a mild summer evening – so warm that Kirsty hadn't bothered with a jacket and was just wearing her favourite pretty floaty summer top, which both flattered curves and, deep green in colour, worked well with her long wavy, auburn hair. Normally so confident and outgoing, especially where boys were concerned, Kirsty found herself feeling oddly nervous – her clammy hands and churning insides making her realise quite how much she liked this quiet, well-mannered boy. As they strolled along the sea-front, talking about nothing in particular, the weather changed and it started to rain. Ever the gentleman, Ben suggested they take shelter on the steps of a grand hotel. It was here, as the warm summer rain came down, looking out over the endless inky blackness of the sea, that Kirsty and her future husband first kissed.

There is a common misconception on Civvy Street that if you marry someone in the military you somehow choose the life and the absences that go with it, that the separations are somehow not as hard for you as they are for a civilian wife whose husband is sent to work away for a few weeks. To say it takes a certain kind of woman to be an army wife is indisputable, but how do you know if you are that woman? I fell in love with Ed despite the fact that he was in the army – and when he left for Iraq after we had been together for eighteen months I waited for him, but, as I tried to explain to friends who would say, wide-eyed, 'I couldn't do it', I had no choice in the matter. I was in love and wasn't going to ditch the man I had given my heart to because he was going away. If I had known how hard it would be when we met, would I have agreed to that second date? Of course – because the good times far outweigh the bad and, as I told my mother when she worried about how I would cope with him away for months at a time, 'I would rather have Ed six months of the year than any other man full time.' Does it make it any easier? Of course not.

'It didn't worry me that he was a soldier,' agrees Julie, 'but I can't stand it when people say to army wives, 'When you marry a soldier you know what you're marrying into.' No you don't. I thought when they're in the army they're home with us – I didn't realise he was going to go to Kosovo, Bosnia, Iraq, Afghanistan – no, I didn't know. I don't think I realised what being an army wife meant for quite a few years.'

Dai had been nothing if not persistent in asking Julie to marry him – it didn't matter how many times she told him to wait, every night he would call from a payphone in his barracks in Ireland and ask her again. The couple hadn't been together long when Julie had fallen pregnant unexpectedly but Dai's mind was made up, he knew she was the woman for him. Just twenty-two, living with her parents in Wales, Julie always gave her boyfriend the same response, 'Just wait till I've had the baby.' Then, when Julie was in her eighth month of pregnancy, something in her clicked and when Dai called, like clockwork, that evening it was Julie's turn to ask, 'Dai, will you marry me?' The couple married immediately and three weeks later their little boy was born.

It was only a few days after her boyfriend Brian had returned from three months in Canada that Kaz found her living room filled with red and white roses, a bottle of champagne and an engagement ring in an open box. For Kaz it was as much of a surprise as falling in love with Brian in the first place. Kaz was divorced and raising a daughter alone, while Brian, the son of a friend, was fifteen years her junior. Kaz never thought for a second that the young soldier would be interested in her, but every weekend Brian would make the two-and-a-half hour drive to Wales to spend the weekend at his mother's and, when Kaz would pop over for her regular cuppa with his mum, the pair would talk. After about a month of this, Brian rang Kaz and asked her out, insisting she met him that evening – the couple dated for a few weeks and when Brian was sent to Canada for three months Kaz agreed to wait for him. Despite sporadic contact, the relationship blossomed, but even so, walking into her living room that day was still a complete shock.

'Is this what I think it is?' Kaz asked, sitting down on the sofa next to Brian.

'Yes,' said Brian.

'Well,' Kaz replied, 'you'd better put the ring on my finger then.'

For Donna and Craig, the decision to get married was one they made together. Despite her assumption that she'd never see him again after that night in the Catterick nightclub, Craig had been true to his word and called her the very next day. After that, jokes Donna, 'I couldn't get rid of him.' Donna wasn't fazed by the fact he was a soldier – it was a world she knew well – and Craig didn't mind that Donna had a three-month-old son by a previous relationship; in fact, he seemed to enjoy playing the role of dad. So getting hitched seemed the logical next step in their relationship.

Donna chose the ring and then waited for the day when Craig would ask her – only hoping he did so somewhere private, and in an understated way, so she wouldn't be embarrassed. In the end they were alone in her mother's sitting room when he got down on one knee – a simple proposal and perfect for Donna. They hadn't been together long, just three months but, with Craig's posting back to the battalion in Tidworth, an imminent marriage was really the only way for the young couple to live together, unmarried soldiers not being able to live with their partners on the patch.

Donna and Craig's wedding was a small one but everyone they wanted to be there was. It was a lovely day, and Donna looked immaculate in a white strapless dress, her brunette hair piled in glossy curls on top of her head and finished with a twinkling tiara. Despite feeling beautiful, Donna, hating to be the centre of attention, was terrified, and desperately tried to stop her knees from knocking as she stood at the altar and made her vows to Craig. The party was less daunting and Donna and Craig had a wonderful evening celebrating with their family and friends. Son Bradley, in contrast to his mum, loved everyone's eyes being on him and spent the night making the guests roar with laughter at his antics. For Donna, the best bit was when everyone had gone, Bradley was with his grandparents, and the couple were on their own for the first time.

And my wedding? I had never been one of those girls that dreamt of a big traditional affair – quite the opposite. In fact I once bet a university friend that I would never, ever walk down the aisle in a white dress. But love changes you and when my boyfriend of eighteen months deployed to Iraq I found myself fantasising about him proposing; the ring, the engagement party and then, as the months went on, the invites, the church, the flowers and, of course, the dress. In my defence – it was far better, and I think healthier, to think about those happy things than to allow the dark thoughts to linger too long in my anxious mind. Long car journeys were the worst – alone, I would start to imagine what I would do if Ed were never to come home and, finding myself in tears, forced the thoughts away, imagining instead seating plans and honeymoon destinations, wedding speeches and first dances.

So I became one of 'those girls' – much to the collective amusement of my friends – and slowly realised that the idea of becoming an army wife was not as remote, or abhorrent, as it once had been. Although I firmly knew that I was in love with Ed, not the army, and resisted the idea (as one well-meaning wife told me) that I was marrying the regiment as well as the man, our wedding day was everything I had daydreamed of and more. I decided that if I was going to marry a soldier I might as well go the whole hog and have all the military paraphernalia we were entitled to. My groom wore his formal Blues uniform and waiting for me on the steps of the church was the guard of honour, made up by sergeant majors from the regiment with whom Ed had served in Iraq, their swords ready to be raised when we left the church as Captain and Mrs Hodges. Ed's Blues looked so impressive; a tailored blue jacket over tight-fitting dark red trousers, shiny black boots with spurs. And with his Iraq medal glinting on his chest he was, every inch, the smart cavalry officer. My bridesmaids wore blue to match him and my shoes – instead of the traditional white – were the deepest shade of midnight blue, again to match my groom.

Walking to the church from my mother's house my stomach churned with nerves, my bridesmaids – three best friends from school and one from university – were laughing and talking but I gripped my father's arm in silence. I had no doubts about marrying Ed, but the emotion of the day was overwhelming. Also, in the back of my mind, there was some apprehension about what would be happening after the wedding – the move to Tidworth and life as an army wife.

It's only once the cake has been cut, the guests have gone and the honeymoon is over that the reality of becoming an army wife really begins to sink in. This is a relationship where your husband's job is going to dictate where and how you live, and where he is going to be, for months at a time, living and fighting in life-threatening situations.

Perhaps that is why Taff decided that the best moment to tell Dereynn that he had decided to join the army was when she was in labour with their second child.

'Shush now,' was Dereynn's response, being more interested in getting through the next wave of contractions than Taff telling her how he was fed up with his current job as a chef.

'Just do whatever,' she said, before completely forgetting the conversation as they celebrated the birth of their son.

But a few weeks later, Taff came home and announced that he had indeed joined up and not only that but his wife was expected to go for an interview.

'I was amazed,' says Dereynn, 'they wanted us to have an interview as a family. They wanted to be sure that we both understood that we would be moving away and check that I would be able to cope with the change.'

Nothing, though, could have prepared Dereynn for her introduction to being an army wife. Taff's initial placement was not in Tidworth, but on the other side of the world, in Hong Kong. The idea of arriving in a completely new country, with no family or friends to support them was very daunting. Laden with baggage and two small children, Taff and Dereynn had struggled on the London Underground en route to the airport. But on their arrival in Hong Kong, the hardest thing was the heat – coming from a cool Liverpool, the muggy humidity of the tropics was a complete shock.

At border control, Taff went through first, leaving Dereynn clutching the handles of her son's buggy and putting a protective arm across the front of her toddler daughter Sian to stop her running to her dad. After what seemed like hours, but must have been only seconds, the passport control official nodded her through and the small family was reunited. 'A horrible moment,' remembers Dereynn, 'but then that was us, in Hong Kong.'

Simone is another Daffodil Girl whose introduction to army life was in Hong Kong. It wasn't just the heat that she remembers, as she stepped from the plane, clutching her five-week-old baby to her chest. It was the wind too – Simone felt as though she was walking into a giant hairdryer, her blonde hair whipping round her face, and sweat pricking the back of her neck. Just seventeen, Simone had never been away from home before – much less flown to a foreign country. She remembers feeling completely alone and terrified.

It was almost immediately after Simone had got married to Mark that he had been posted to Hong Kong. The couple, with their families, had travelled up to Gatwick the week before – but an army error with Simone's passport meant that the young mother and son had to stay behind and let Mark fly to Hong Kong alone. Simone had to travel all the way back to Wales and return, a week later, to board a plane for the first time in her life – and on her own.

'I had never left my family before,' remembers Simone, 'they took me to the airport – everybody was crying and I was so scared. My mother was saying to the British Airways stewardess, 'Please look after my daughter,' and she was crying too. I got on the plane on my own – I can't believe how brave I was in those days.'

Thousands of miles from home, it was the first time the couple had lived together. 'It was exciting and hard,' says Simone, 'and in some ways, being so far from home was good – when you're learning to live together, you find out each other's faults, but if we did have a little argument, we only had each other, we couldn't run home to our mums. In my head I felt very grown-up and capable but when I look back now I wonder if I really was.'

Julie's new husband, Dai, meanwhile, was stationed in Ireland. Julie and their son continued to live with her parents while they waited for a married quarter to become available. When the baby was three weeks old, Dai drove over to pick up his family. For Julie there were mixed emotions; she was in love and wanted her own home but at the same time dreaded leaving her mum and dad, sister and brother. They had all helped so much with the new baby and the thought of coping on her own was terrifying – the day Dai drove her away from her mum and dad's was one of the worst of the young wife's life.

For Kaz, Kirsty and Donna, life as Daffodil Girls began on the patch in Tidworth, though with somewhat different emotions for each of them. Peering through the window of the empty house, Kaz and Brian couldn't believe their luck; 'We felt as though we'd won the lottery,' Kaz says. The couple had got married a year previously but decided there was no point in Kaz and her daughter uprooting themselves and moving to Germany where Brian was then stationed. Tidworth, then, was to be their first home together. Brand new, with three bedrooms and a garden, the detached house was nicer than anything Kaz had imagined.

When Kirsty first saw her new house, it looked so bare she struggled to imagine it as a home at all. She had been married to Benedict for less than a week, and had no idea of what to expect. Looking round the three-bedroomed semi, Kirsty couldn't help but focus on the unattractive features: the frosted glass window on the hatch between the dining room and kitchen; the horrid doors and awful army curtains; the army-issue sofas, the only furniture in the house, were uncomfortable and plain.

It was only once they began to unpack that it started to feel like theirs. 'The kitchen's very nice, with all cream tones and light wood; I arranged my red and cream canisters and immediately it looked like a decorated room – a proper "designed" room,' Kirsty says. 'In the living room, as soon as we got a coffee table from IKEA, a TV and TV stand and put our mirror up, it looked much better. It didn't take much work for it to look more homely and I'm proud of what we've done. Before the wedding people would say to me, "You haven't even lived together yet – what if you can't get on?" But it's just been completely harmonious – we work like a team. Neither of us is really finicky or house-proud, but we're both respectful of each other's space and we love being together.'

Donna and Craig had been living together in Donna's one-bedroom flat in Catterick since they had got engaged, so moving in together in Tidworth wasn't a new thing. There wasn't much money, but they enjoyed doing what they could to smarten up the three-bedroomed property, buying their own curtains and blinds to make the place more like their own home. Soon after moving, Craig told Donna the news she was dreading – that he would be going away within the year. Donna had known that doing a tour at some point was inevitable, but had hoped they would have had more time together as newlyweds before he left. In those early days, stuck at home with a small child, Donna found it quite lonely and boring: her phone bill rocketed as she spent endless hours speaking to family and friends back in Catterick. Craig encouraged his young wife to go to coffee mornings to meet other wives, but Donna felt shy and worried that the wives of the higher-ranking soldier's would be cliquey. And even when she did start venturing out and making friends, Donna could never escape the thought that when Craig went away, Tidworth really wouldn't feel like home.

The anxieties of the Daffodil Girls at starting their new lives are ones that I can remember only too well. My own patch life began on a typical November morning; cold, grey and drizzling with the kind of rain that makes you feel chilled to your core. The house was chaos. Boxes dumped unceremoniously everywhere, piles of newspaper where unpacking had been started and abandoned, the furniture in all the wrong places. Quite simply, it was completely overwhelming. I stepped out of the back door into the garden; the impressive-sized lawn was covered in a mush of decomposing autumn leaves and the dull sound of car tyres on wet tarmac was clearly audible from the busy through road just beyond the fence that backed the garden. I lit a cigarette, my hand shaking slightly, as I surveyed my new home. I loved my new husband but I really did not want to be here.

It had been a stressful few days – barely taking time to draw breath after returning from honeymoon, I was tasked with packing up our little home in Bath and moving, reluctantly, to Tidworth. Unlike many newly-wed army couples, Ed and I had lived together before getting married, buying a tiny terraced Georgian cottage the year before in my childhood home city. I had fallen in love with the cottage at first look and persuaded Ed that we could manage a life there with him commuting to Tidworth and me spending a few days a week in London. Ed proposed on the doorstep the day we got the keys and we had an idyllic year playing house together. But the commute was a lot to ask – just over an hour each way daily – and, as I had stopped working for a newspaper in London, the logical thing was to take advantage of the low rent and take an army quarter. That cold first morning, however, it was hard to remember the positive reasons why we had left my dream home and moved to an army garrison town. Standing there with my cigarette, I didn't want to go inside and yet, with the distant crump of artillery from the ranges on Salisbury Plain, outside was not a comforting option either.

Then the doorbell rang. It was one of my new neighbours, a wife I had known when she and I were both girlfriends hanging out at mess parties and emailing one another when our boys were away. She presented me with a beautiful purple orchid and card welcoming me to the patch. Over a cup of tea, we talked for about fifteen minutes and by the time she left I suddenly didn't feel so alone any more. Over the course of the next few days, as the wives' club geared itself up, cards, flowers and even champagne were dropped off to welcome Ed and I to our new home. It seemed I had been wrong about Tidworth, and realised it was time to get to know it better.

CHAPTER 2

'The Place We Army Couples Call Home'

Ed and I had known each other for only a few weeks when I first visited Tidworth. It was early evening and as we drove into town, even through the gathering shadows, I could tell immediately that this was not the most beautiful of places. I didn't think for a moment this might be somewhere I could end up living – at this point I didn't even dream that Ed and I would be anything more than a fun interlude before he went away at Christmas, skiing with the army for six weeks. So, as we passed through the armed guard at the main gate and drove through the barbed-wire enclosed barracks to Ed's mess, the building where an unmarried officer lived and socialised, I found it all rather exciting; there were real live soldiers with guns, tanks and a building steeped in history – filled with silver, paintings and handsome young men in uniform.

As our relationship continued and started to get more serious, I would visit Tidworth as often as possible – driving down mid-week after work only to rise at the crack of dawn the next day, slogging through rush-hour traffic to get back before my working day began. I loved coming to Tidworth, but only because Ed was there. We would have 'carpet picnics' in Ed's room because really there was nowhere else to go, nothing else to do, so we sat on the floor by his two single, army-issue beds. I would take food with me (a Spar being the only food shop in Tidworth at this point) or we would treat ourselves to a Chinese meal from the slightly sad takeaway on the shopping high street, flicking through greasy back copies of the *Daily Star* newspaper while we waited for our food.

In 2007 a branch of Tesco opened, and I remember telling Ed that I could marry him now, as there would be somewhere I could do my shopping. Despite the joke, the potential location for the start of our married life did put me off, or at least give me something to complain about once we got engaged. I have always been spoilt by the places I have lived: I was brought up in the Georgian city of Bath and glamorous Notting Hill in London, and grew up being used to beautiful buildings as standard. After university, I moved into a tiny flat in Ladbroke Grove – it wasn't picturesque, but the nearby cosmopolitan bustle of Portobello and Golborne Roads made it a great place to live. When Ed and I moved to Bath, a year before getting married, we loved our life there because there was so much to do and see – exhibitions, theatre, bars and restaurants; on any given night of the week there would be a million and one options open to us. We knew that when we moved to Tidworth, despite its size, this would not be the case.

There is no escaping Tidworth's long connection with battle – even before the army took it over at the end of the nineteenth century; the beautiful landscape encircling the town is dominated by the Iron Age hill fort Sidbury Hill, as well as a complicated system of defensive earthworks. Then there are the barrows and tumuli where those killed in battle up to three thousand years ago are buried.

To the casual observer Tidworth might look like any other nondescript country town or suburb. But the place we army couples call home – for a while at least – is an artificial creation that would not exist were it not for the British Army. Two separate villages with slightly different names, North Tidworth in Wiltshire and South Tedworth in Hampshire, were engulfed to make one when, in 1897, the War Office bought the estate and Tedworth House itself. It was the army that created the town we now know, and the names of the barracks built to accommodate the men were given the names of famous battles fought in India and Afghanistan: Jallalabad, Kandahar, Assaye and Aliwal, among others.

You have only to walk through the town's military cemetery or visit either of the two garrison churches to realise what an effect all the wars and conflicts of the twentieth and twenty-first centuries have had on Tidworth. For more than a hundred years, British regiments have left the town to travel and fight around the world, with all too many men returning only to lie beneath its soil. Today,

Tidworth (together with neighbouring Bulford) is home to 1 Mechanised Brigade and 12 Mechanised Brigade. The first comprises 2 Royal Tank Regiment, the Daffodil Girls' 2 Royal Welsh (armoured infantry), 1st Regiment Royal Horse Artillery and 6th Battalion Royal Electrical and Mechanical Engineers (REME); the second comprises the King's Royal Hussars (my husband's regiment), 19 Regiment Royal Artillery, and 4 Battalion REME. Stationed close by are further elements of the two brigades, as well as Engineers, Rifles and some smaller units.

All these names carry with them history and loyalty – guaranteed to prompt feelings of pride in those who are a part of the whole. Yet this regimented place is also home to a shifting community of families. The population of about 16,000 is never static – about one-third will leave and be replaced each year. It has, too, a very high proportion of families with young children, whose soldier-fathers may be absent for six months or more in a year. After a few months of living here I realised that I rarely spotted anyone over the age of fifty. Soldiers have to retire at forty-five and officers, of whom there are fewer, might only stay on until their mid-fifties.

Sitting at my desk, I will frequently hear helicopters whirring overhead and from the window watch tanks trundling past on the road beyond our garden – the sounds of war are now as familiar to me as the screech of police sirens were when I lived in Ladbroke Grove. Tidworth is a town whose army influence is impossible to ignore: when an exercise brings the men into town, we wives become used to walking past groups of soldiers, covered in cam paint, on our way to the supermarket. Up on the plain, you will often encounter groups of men hiding in the trees or marching with full backpack, clutching rifles – soldiers who studiously ignore you and continue their boyish yet so-serious war games. They used to give me a fright, but these days I just smile at the somewhat surreal world in which I now live.

The villages of Tidworth, North Tidworth and South Tedworth may be joined as one these days, but echoes of the old divide still linger into the present day. For Tidworth is a town split in two along army lines: South Tidworth is where the officers live, while North Tidworth is for the regular soldiers.

My road is one lived in by officers: most of whom are captains. The houses are detached with a good space between each one and green verges, trees and hedgerows make it one of the prettier parts of Tidworth. Over the fairly busy byway, opposite our road, is the sports oval and a beautiful tree-lined park leading to Tedworth House, one of the most lovely nineteenth-century country houses in Wiltshire, and the polo pitches which are overlooked by four imposing generals' houses.

Our street is not a through road; it leads, instead, to the wooded outskirts of Salisbury Plain and the grand expanse of plain beyond. A breathless walk to the top provides a bird's-eye view of the town: from this vantage point, Tidworth is spread at your feet. To the left is another street, running parallel, with four cul-de-sacs leading off it, each with between six and ten houses. Although close, these houses are very different to ours: smaller and attached, they house a range of ranks from junior captains and lieutenants to warrant officers. This is where Kirsty and Ben live.

To the right of my street, also running parallel, is another road, and here the houses are different again. A single row facing a small wood, the houses are bigger and smarter. They are mainly home to colonels, and have five bedrooms and gated driveways. For officers, the number of bedrooms you get is in direct proportion to what rank you are – below captain it is two and a half, captain three, major four, colonel five and above that five or six plus. Below officer rank, the number of bedrooms are allocated in a seemingly more logical way, decided according to how many children the family has.

A short walk a little further into town is the new Tesco – the kind of mega-superstore that small communities often complain about but couldn't be more popular here in Tidworth. Before its arrival, the nearest decent supermarket was in Andover, a half-hour drive each way, which meant an entire afternoon could be eaten up shopping. The superstore has also brought jobs to the area – I know more than one army wife who works there. For me, the fact that I can pop up the road for food, wine and household essentials makes me feel less isolated – reminding me of the ease of my old life in London.

Nine times out of ten you will bump into people you know while shopping: I'm used to soldiers saluting my husband and wives stopping to say hello. This can be lovely, but when you're hung-over and tired, dressed in your tracksuit and Ugg boots, the last thing you want is to bump into someone you almost know and have to make small talk. Before I moved to the patch, one woman told me of her horror of shopping in Tesco when she was being anything less than a 'perfect wife': she was convinced that the other wives would be peering into her basket and judging the number of ready meals and bottles of wine. Another told me that she still made the round trip to Andover on occasion for certain items after bumping into two wives from her husband's regiment when she had a pregnancy test ill-concealed in her trolley. The questions were well-meaning and enthusiastic, but, as the couple in question were struggling to conceive, very unwelcome.

Tesco is on Station Road, the main shopping 'hub' for Tidworth and the natural dividing line between north and South Tidworth. There is also, among other businesses, a Lidl supermarket, a dentist, a pizza takeaway, a bookie, a hairdressing salon, a craft shop, two veterinary clinics, a photographic studio and – the most recent addition – a smart Indian restaurant (the opening of which was cause for massive excitement on the patch). It is not a road where you would meet friends to go shopping and no comparison to the high street in Marlborough, the nearest town which is almost the same size as Tidworth.

Before I embarked on writing this book I hadn't explored the sprawling estates of Zouch and Matthews in North Tidworth, having driven through only once when a corporal's wife from my husband's regiment kindly gave me a lift home after a wives 'do' and dropped three women off there first before me. Rebuilt in the noughties, Matthews is the newer of the estates: it is here that the majority of the

Daffodil Girls live. The estate is predominantly made up of attached small houses consisting of three bedrooms with a garden; it is very close-knit with lots of pedestrian-only areas. Children run around playing with their neighbours, their friends, and I was struck, when I went there to talk to the Daffodil Girls, by the sense of community – a place where, if you live there, everyone really does know your name. Zouch is much older: a remnant of the Sixties council estates you would find anywhere in the UK, with slightly worn blocks of flat and houses that remind me of the less salubrious parts of Ladbroke Grove, the irony being that if you were living in London, many young professionals would jump at the chance of living in a house or flat like these, were the location right.

One person who has seen all sides of life in Tidworth is Amanda. Amanda moved to Tidworth from Germany in 2005, along with her husband Lee and their two children, Megan and Bethan. They lived on the Matthews estate, which had been rebuilt a couple of years earlier, and now, five years on, they live in South Tidworth – a stone's throw from me – in a captain's quarter identical to mine and Ed's. Amanda and Lee were married when he was a corporal and she has been by his side as he was promoted to sergeant, colour sergeant major and then, at the end of his tour of Iraq in 2007 and two years earlier than normal, to officer – a captain. This means that the couple have experienced all kinds of army housing throughout Lee's career. 'I love living in our new house, it is like being an army wife with all the benefits but without being too immersed in patch life,' Amanda says. 'We have a huge garden, which is a bit redundant at our age, something we could have done with when the kids were younger and it is so quiet and peaceful compared to living on the Matthews estate. The houses there are much newer but they have walls like paper and you really do live on top of your neighbours.'

In the Matthews and Zouch estates – unlike the officers' quarters – different ranks of soldiers can live alongside one another as houses are allocated according to size of the family rather than rank. So Kaz, married to a lance corporal, lives in the same area as Dereynn, a sergeant's wife, and Mandy and Simone, both married to sergeant majors. 'It used to be different,' Amanda tells me, 'so that as you moved up the ranks you could expect to get a better house, but when the battalion was in Germany they changed it and you got what you were given, typically just as Lee and I were going to be entitled to a better house.'

Amanda finds Tidworth far more convenient than other patches she has lived in – it is near enough to Wales to make family visits easy and her daughters are doing their GCSEs and A-levels at a brand new secondary school just fifteen minutes away. For the couple, moving to an officer's house in South Tidworth was a good moment in their army career. Amanda didn't care about the status of having a bigger home, nor did it occur to her that she would be in South, rather than North, Tidworth: she was just thrilled to be away from the closeness of the Matthews estate, to have more privacy. Speaking to her made me realise how fortunate Ed and I are to have the same house and location for our first married home as Amanda and Lee do after eighteen years in the army. To me, a Londoner who never knew any of my neighbours' names, my street can feel claustrophobic, with everyone knowing everyone's business – but I realise now how private it is compared to the other housing options in Tidworth.

Amanda describes the stage she and Lee are in now as being in 'no-man's land' – her husband is not the same as a direct entry (DE) Officer (someone like Ed, who attended Sandhurst to enter the army with the rank of officer immediately). Lee is older, and more experienced than the DE captains and Amanda, too, at a different stage in her life from the comparable wives. She and Lee are also now a stage away from their previous peer group – only allowed in the sergeants' mess when invited and slightly removed from the community in which they used to play such a big part. By Amanda's own admission, even at officers' dos the late entry (LE) officers can be a bit of clique, sticking together and, not having the same shared history, not really choosing to socialise with other officer couples outside of the mess.

Amanda finds 'no-man's land', in many ways, a relief – she feels a sense of freedom, knowing she can do things without all her neighbours knowing – or caring. 'I have lost touch with lots of people,' she says, 'it is no one's fault and really it is up to me to maintain friendships. However, the tried and tested ones I have taken with me. Living a bit further away from everyone else I have become a bit invisible. When Lee was RSM [regimental sergeant major, the most senior soldier in the battalion] and we lived in Matthews, I had people knocking on the door all the time, ringing all the time. I was massively involved in the welfare side of the battalion. But when Lee handed over, I handed over to the new wife too. So I didn't really mind being slightly removed from it all – it was good to have some peace and quiet.'

The 2nd Battalion The Royal Welsh is a new battalion but one with a long history; it is also a battalion that has seen much in the way of warfare in recent years. Amanda's Lee is one of the longer-serving soldiers and his medals reflect this. 'He's got seven or eight medals now – a fair old chestful,' Amanda says. 'We have a gallery in our warrant officers' and sergeants' mess of past regimental sergeant majors [RSMs] through the years, which goes back to the Sixties – so you see all these RSMs in line, and most of them have one medal. These are men at the end of their army service, and the medal they have is their Northern Ireland, or their Long Service and GC [Good Conduct] medal. Then, as the line gets fresher and newer, and the pictures look a little less dated, the medals start to stretch across the chest. It shows what the army has gone through in the last twenty years.'

Created on St David's Day, 2006, The Royal Welsh is an amalgamation of Royal Welch Fusiliers and the Royal Regiment of Wales, creating three battalions – The 1st and 2nd and a Territorial Army The Royal Welsh. Both original regiments can trace their lineage back more than three hundred years. The 2 R Welsh, in its previous and current incarnation and inclusive of both First and Second World Wars, has seen active service at Waterloo and in Egypt, Africa, America, the Balkans, Northern Ireland, Iraq and Afghanistan, among others. Historically, the battalion's most famous battle honour was in defence of Rorke's Drift, South Africa, during the Zulu campaign in January 1879. The battle is remarkable because the greatest number of Victoria Crosses was awarded for a single engagement (eleven). The story was immortalised in the 1964 film *Zulu*, staring Michael Caine.

To be a Daffodil Girl in recent years has been to follow your husband around the world. The longest-serving Daffodil Girl, Simone, married her soldier when the battalion was stationed in Hong Kong. Since then, she has been stationed in Shropshire, Northern Ireland and Germany before settling in Tidworth in 2005. The battalion is 98 per cent Welsh but amongst the Daffodil Girls are women from Liverpool, North Yorkshire and Shropshire. The other battalion of The Royal Welsh, the 1st, is currently stationed in Chester and there is a friendly rivalry between the two despite the shared history.

There is, as I have mentioned, not much to do in Tidworth. There is one pub set between the two estates of Zouch and Matthew but The Ram is not somewhere I have ever visited. There is an unwritten rule that officers keep out of the pub, leaving it for the more junior ranks to enjoy.

Officers instead tend to make the fifteen-minute drive to a gastro pub near Tidworth – The Mallet Arms, in Newton Toney – where, on any given night of the week, you will find single officers getting away from the mess for a night and married army couples on a date enjoying the relative civilisation of a meal out. The men are almost all dressed in the mufti outfit for officers of smart jeans or cords and a shirt (normally pink or blue checked) and tucking into the Mallet speciality – The Mallet Burger.

Other than the two pubs, socialising in Tidworth mostly takes place in people's home or in the mess. Each regiment or battalion has three messes – one for officers, one for sergeants and one for corporals. The messes are behind the wire in camp and, although wives and girlfriends are often invited, are very much a male domain. Here the single men live, eat, sleep and socialise, with the married soldiers joining them for lunches, mess dinner night and parties. In my relatively brief army career as girlfriend, and now wife, one of my favourite parts of this strange world is parties and dinners in the officers' mess – they have an other-worldly feel to them and as a modern young woman, used to past dates who would jump at the chance to split the bill and never dream of holding the door open for you, there is something wonderful in the old-fashioned formality of the set table, the traditions, the fact that the man next to you will always pull out your chair.

Ed's regiment moved its officers' mess in 2007 from its turn-of-the-nineteenth-century home to a newly constructed building just up the road. Although far more comfortable, with decent heating and facilities, this new mess doesn't have quite the same gravitas as the old one. The 2 R Welsh is rightfully proud of its officers' mess – out of eight similar buildings in Tidworth, it is only one of two which is listed – and instead of moving, the battalion has done up the interior, giving the same level of comfort but keeping the style. Built in 1905, Lucknow, as it is named, is

41

on the edge of camp overlooking a public field and it is very impressive.

The officers' mess dos I have attended tend to be formal events, with women expected to wear below-the-knee dresses and cover their shoulders, so I was surprised when Amanda told me that compared to the sergeants' mess, she found the officers' mess comparatively lax with its rules and regulations. Amanda has lived through all three – corporals', sergeants' and now officers' messes and she tells me that the rules are far stricter in the sergeants' than the other two. 'There is a much stricter mess etiquette,' she explains, 'for example, ladies are not allowed to go the bar unaccompanied; you sit at table until told you are allowed to get up. Men are not allowed to the toilet during the meal. It is taken seriously because when you reach the rank of sergeant it is something you have earned and the men like the gravitas of the traditions and history that goes with that rank to continue. It is different in the corporals' mess because the men are younger, and more junior, and I suppose that same reasoning applies to the officers' mess – the young men living in are in their early and mid-twenties; bound to be a bit more rowdy than older, married sergeants even though technically the officers' rank is senior.'

For Amanda, living with strict mess etiquette for more than thirteen years, she was shocked by the different attitude in the officers' mess. 'Everything is focused on having a really good time, the rules are much more relaxed,' she says. 'From an LE perspective, we were surprised the young officers could behave how they did and nobody blinked an eyelid other than me and other LE wives. It was a mess ball and they had hired a rodeo; one of the young officer's girlfriends hitched up her evening dress to have a go and we were shocked to see she wasn't wearing any knickers. She came flying off, legs akimbo, and we couldn't believe it. None of us LE wives would have dreamed of hitching up an evening dress to get up there, even when we were young wives going to the corporals' mess – and with no underwear on. I whispered to a friend, "I'm wearing enough knickers for the two of us" (surreptitiously readjusting my "Trinny", as we call them, support pants), and we just fell about laughing. I've got used to the difference now but I still hold back – the etiquette I learned is now embedded, I suppose. I do miss it slightly, the regimented sequence of mess dos in the sergeants' mess, because you knew where you were, where you stood.'

Unlike in the real world, army couples do not get to pick the house they will be living in for the next few years. Even though they will be paying rent (minimal but a rent none the less) they are not able to look at a potential selection of homes, but instead are allocated a 'quarter' as they call it in army land – as in living quarter. You are allowed one refusal, a refusal that Ed and I used almost immediately when we were offered a house on a road in which, I had pre-warned Ed, I would categorically not live – if I was going to give up our home in Bath I wanted us to live in the best possible option in Tidworth.

Second time round we got lucky: aware that a couple from Ed's regiment were moving out, we put in a bid for their house, which was both on the road we wanted to live on and going to be empty at the right time. We knew the inside of the houses on the street fairly well; good friends of ours had moved there two years previously and, believe me, if you have been to one house on our street, you really have been to them all. They are identical – thirty-one 1950s-build houses on either side of the road. Tiled roofs and red tile cladding covering the top half of the house, with the bottom half-painted a tired shade of cream. Inside the layout is the same: downstairs is a small entrance hall, kitchen, utility room, dining room; upstairs, plonked on top like a child's doll house, are three bedrooms and a bathroom and separate loo, each room exactly the same size as the corresponding room below it. The walls are painted magnolia and the fittings and features rather show their age now but (mostly) are practical and functional. I say all the houses are identical, but in fact some are in reverse, with the kitchen and back door on the opposite side to ours with everything else mirrored accordingly – after a few glasses of wine at a neighbour's it can get very confusing.

You can paint the rooms, as long as you return them to their neutral magnolia before handing the house back. We haven't bothered – I am too lazy to paint a home I am only in short-term – and instead have filled the house with art and photographs. The walls of the room where I write are a patchwork of postcards and clippings and the upstairs loo sports a bright collage of photographs from our life together. Anything to put your stamp on your home, to make it different from your neighbours', is worth doing: there is no greater compliment to pay an army wife than to say, 'Your house doesn't look like an army house at all.'

Regulations allow one hook per wall – a rule that is almost universally ignored, leading to frantic use of Polyfilla in the days leading up to a 'march out' to hide the telltale holes in the plaster. 'March in' and 'march out' are the terms used to describe the handover of the house – as new tenants you check the house before accepting the keys; the housing people check it before they take back their keys. Just as with renting anywhere, you are expected to receive and return a quarter that is spotless throughout.

Sadly, this is not always the case – but as Amanda tells me, life on the patch means there is always someone who will help you out. 'This house, when we got it, was a total state inside – dirty, greasy, not up to march-out standard at all. I was bitterly disappointed and had to spend the first day just scrubbing and scrubbing. I was working full-time at Help for Heroes and only took one day off work, so there just wasn't enough time to make the house nice for Lee and the kids and also get our old house up to scratch to be handed back. My friends knew I was struggling so one day Dereynn, Julie and Tracey met me at the old house and we blitzed it in one evening. Julie kept the keys and went there the following day with Tracey and got it to march-out standard. That is real friendship – rank and geography doesn't change that.'

CHAPTER 3

'I Came Across As A Lost Little Girl'

The battalion had pulled out all the stops for the officers' Christmas party. It was being held in the main room of the Edwardian officers' mess; the flickering candles, linen-draped tables groaning with the battalion silver and oil portraits on the walls giving the impression of the dining hall of a grand estate. Ben looked smart in black tie and Kirsty was in her favourite outfit: a Monsoon black silk empire-line dress with bow detailing on the back, with black satin shoes adorned with roses. Her hair was falling in loose waves around her face and her subtly-applied make-up made her blue eyes stand out. Kirsty felt beautiful but was still feeling nervous, gripping Ben's hand tightly as they walked into the room.

There were around 120 people at the party – officers from 2 Royal Welsh and their wives or girlfriends – and it was the first time Kirsty had really met any of them: Benedict was new to the battalion and the couple had only moved to the patch a couple of weeks before. Benedict was extremely young to be married for an officer, and on the table of junior officers where he and Kirsty were seated, it soon became apparent they were the only married couple.

The table looked beautiful – as smart as any wedding table Kirsty had seen before – and she was thrilled by her name card, a crisp white rectangle bearing, for the first time, her married name. She made a note to slip it into her handbag later as a keepsake. There were party favours for the female guests too and Kirsty was pleased by her Cath Kidson lip-gloss.

As wine was poured and dinner was served – a joint of pork and beef per table – Kirsty felt her nerves disappearing and her confidence starting to grow. Talking to the other officers and their guests, Kirsty was starting to enjoy the knowledge that the other girls were just dates, and that she was the only wife. They were all as new as she was to the battalion, but being married meant Kirsty was the only one living on the patch. Somehow, this gave her more standing, and even though she had only been living there a few weeks, the other girls were fascinated to know what living in this strange new world was like.

After dinner, too much amusement and laughter, two officers dressed as Father Christmas and his helper elf came out to give joke presents – items like a bin and cleaning fluid to one senior officer who was particularly fussy about the younger men keeping their rooms clean. Ben was one of those called up, and Kirsty blushed crimson as she watched her husband be made to sit on Father Christmas's knee. Ben was given a bottle of champagne to congratulate him on finding a wife, and a packet of painkillers for the headache that same new wife would undoubtedly cause him. 'It was all very good-natured though,' remembers Kirsty.

As the alcohol flowed, things became more relaxed, culminating in all of the tables joining in to sing one verse each from the festive song *The Twelve Days of Christmas*. 'It was brilliant,' says Kirsty. 'They started with the more junior ranks' tables – including ours – all of whom were quite reserved. But as we got further down the song, and higher up the ranks, people were giving it their all, standing on chairs and tables and really belting their verse out. After dinner the bar stayed open till the early hours and I got the chance to get to know some more people and found the other wives very friendly. It was,' she remembers with a smile, 'a great introduction to patch life.'

If any of the girlfriends on Kirsty's table had quizzed me about what patch life was like after my first couple of weeks, I'm not sure that I would have been quite so positive about the experience. I have to be honest – I struggled in my first few months as an army wife. My beloved grandmother died within a week of us moving to our new home and, although she was well into her nineties so it was not unexpected, a light definitely went out in the world. With the miserable winter weather closing in and Ed's departure for two months' training imminent, and the glow of the wedding and honeymoon starting to fade, I was not a happy newlywed.

Salvation for me came in two different ways. The first was of the four-legged variety. I had wanted a dog for ages and it was one of the incentives Ed used to persuade me that the move to Tidworth was a good idea. Ed had originally wanted to wait – he knew he would be going away for two months' training in January and was worried about me coping alone in Tidworth with the new house and a new puppy. But my mind was made up – a few days of living on the patch and with Ed's absence looming I knew I needed something, a living creature, to love and look after other than my husband.

On a cold Sunday morning, Ed agreed to drive down to Devon to 'look at' some eight-week-old puppies. I think Ed knew in his heart of hearts that there wasn't a chance in hell of us driving away empty-handed but we both pretended that was a possibility as we sped down the A303 to meet what would become the newest member of our family.

At the breeders, surrounded by impossibly sweet Labradoodle puppies, Ed was quickly won over and Freddie joined our life and immediately made a difference. As a new wife on the patch, without a job to go to, it was all too easy to pull the duvet up over my head and ignore the day – Freddie soon put a stop to that, getting me out of the bed at the crack of dawn and making me laugh with his constant play.

The other salvation came in the form of a senior officer's wife. As Kirsty was also to discover, the warmth of welcome from the army wives is never far away. Not long after Freddie's arrival, the wife of Ed's commanding officer arranged to come and see me, meet the puppy and take me to my first coffee morning. I was a little apprehensive – this was the wife of my husband's boss, and although I had met her before and thought she was lovely I couldn't help but be conscious of boxes still unpacked, the pile of wine bottles in the recycling bin and puppy-induced chaos in our kitchen.

As it turned out, any concerns I might have had were completely misplaced. Tina is one of those women you can't help but like – and she arrived laden with chocolates and flowers and brimming with enthusiasm. Full of sympathy about my grandmother and praise for my new puppy she broke through my 'newbie' gloom in seconds. Petite, with long dark hair and a mouth that is always smiling, Tina is not a twin-set-and-pearls kind of army wife, instead always dressing fashionably with a bit of a twist. Her denim jacket with a hawk embroidered on the back (the symbol of the regiment) was infamous across the patch – her husband's soldiers loving the obvious pride she felt for the King's Royal Hussars.

When Tina's husband became a commanding officer he wasn't the only one with a new set of responsibilities. While he was taking over command of the regiment, Tina took over the running of the wives' club with equal gusto. Under her keen eye, coffee mornings became better attended, a wives' Christmas party was organised and every new wife was welcomed to life as a 'wife of' a King's Royal Hussar. It didn't matter whether your husband was a trooper or a major – Tina greeted them all with equal friendliness.

The coffee morning was not quite as glamorous an introduction to my fellow regimental wives as Kirsty's Christmas party had been. It was held in a hall near the medical centre, and I entered to the sight of clusters of wives standing talking while children of varying ages ran around fully free-range. This was the first time I had been to something like this and I was every bit as nervous as Kirsty – but at least she had her husband next to her for support.

Tina wasn't having any of my shyness – introducing me to soldiers' wives and children, joining me for a cigarette outside, and generally going out of her way to make me feel comfortable and at home. Everyone was very welcoming, though I couldn't help noticing that the ranking of my husband made some of the greetings a little more cautious: some of the wives of the more junior ranks seemed as shy to speak to me as I was to them.

I suspect that might be the case for any large organisation – the wife of a runner for a television company might be shy to share a cup of tea with one of the producer's partners – but even so, something about it being the army made it feel a bit different. I was aware that it should be up to me to break this stalemate, but wasn't sure how. This clearly wasn't something that troubled Tina: although her husband was the equivalent of the CEO, every single person there was comfortable with her and she with them. Whatever life Tina had ended up in, you just know she would have spent it making those around her as happy as possible – the role of commanding officer's wife was made for her.

As with Kirsty, my first group event felt a little daunting, but from then on my life on the patch really began. I got to know various wives who lived on our road, as well as pursuing friendships with those women I had known when we were girlfriends and socialised at mess dos and in London. All went out of their way to invite me for tea, say hi as they passed and generally be more welcoming than any neighbour would ever be out in the real world. These were the sort of neighbours you could borrow emergency supplies from when halfway through a meal, or would be happy to go out dog walking (and wife talking) together. Ed and I had our first couple of dinner parties, mixing married couples with guys who still lived in the mess – I loved laying the table with our wedding china and trying to emulate the hostess my mother had been when I was growing up. It was all part of learning to be a wife and an army one at that.

One of the strangest sights in the life of an army wife is watching your husband leave for work in the morning. Dressed in his combat gear, Ed would leave on the dot of 8.15 for the fifteen-minute cycle to work. I would watch from the landing window and observe our domestic scene being repeated up and down the road, and no doubt on every other street in the town. It might not sound much but it's a very powerful image: the soldiers leaving for work, dressed in their combat uniform, beret firmly on, the wives watching them go – a daily reminder that we're part of something bigger, that we're all in this together.

This shared sense of community can make you feel as though you've stepped back in time to the Fifties and at times it can seem as though Wisteria Lane is not just some fictional television setting. On bad days, the ones when you close the door to your empty house and pine for the life you've given up, it can all feel a little too close for comfort. But a friendly smile from a neighbour and a husband returning home for lunch would soon banish any lingering concerns.

For Kirsty, living somewhere where everyone knew everyone reminded her a little of being at home. 'All my family are situated in one little village; my nan lives next door but one, and my auntie is on the other side – we'll just go and nick milk off each other without even necessarily saying we're in the house. In a way it is a bit like patch life because you know your neighbours – I know there are people nearby who would help me out if I asked.'

It wasn't long before the officers' wives' club was inviting Kirsty to join them for a range of social occasions. 'They were lovely,' says Kirsty, 'really welcoming, warm and friendly but I couldn't help feeling as though I came across as a lost little girl – they all had children starting school and had things like that in common and they were married to men more senior than my husband. I felt a little bit intimidated, out of my comfort zone, but that was my issue not theirs. I guess it is something that will come in time. After all, I am the only lieutenant's wife in battalion, I am not sure even if any of the captains are married; the wives I met had all had a lot longer to get used to army life than me.'

For some of these other Daffodil Girls, living on the patch had been a way of life they had learnt to love over many years. 'I like the security it provides more than anything else,' says Amanda. 'My children go to school just up the road – they've got friends within the regiment that they've known since they were born.'

Having been a Daffodil Girl for many years, Amanda had spent time not just on the patch in Britain, but had also experienced life as an army wife out in Germany. Here, if anything, the feeling of togetherness was even stronger. 'It's a little travelling community – a little commune,' she explains. 'Even when we were in Germany, you could shut your front door and be anywhere in the world, but you open it and go out, and you see your friends, and you could be in Wales. It doesn't matter where you are, because you're all together.'

Rhiannon also has fond memories of patch life abroad. 'In Germany, in the bosom of the army, it's a bit like here – but more so. You are completely subsumed into the army life.' Rhiannon worked for the brigade headquarters while she was out there. 'I loved that – Huw was away most of the four years that we lived in Germany but having a job made it far more bearable. I made friends at work and through our neighbours; when Huw was away I would hang out with all my friends and go round people's houses, and there was a couple who basically fed me four nights a week.'

Rhiannon really noticed the closeness of patch life when Huw's job took them away from the Daffodil Girls, 'We then had five years away from the battalion, and being away from it is a different kettle of fish. While you always make good friends, it's not that close-knit thing. I didn't know if it was just because I wasn't in Germany, or not with the battalion, but there was a distance – a separation.'

When Huw returned to 2 Royal Welsh, Rhiannon was both pleased to return to the community feel, and also worried that it might have disappeared in the interim. 'Coming back to the battalion, and Huw going on tour for the first time in five years, I wondered, "What if it was not the same – what if I don't cope as well as before, if I don't have that close-knit thing?" We'd been away a long time and it was going to be different people on the patch – I was worried it wouldn't be the same as Germany.' Rhiannon paused, then added, 'And this war's different now.'

I was struck by how important Rhiannon's job at brigade headquarters had been to her. The benefits of finding army-related work are twofold: it gives you the satisfaction of doing something both useful and supportive of your husband's work, and also strengthens that feeling that you are part of something, and that you belong.

This is something that I understood from my own experiences. I still remember vividly the day that I drove my mini over the country potholes en route to Salisbury, on my way to the trading offices of the charity Help for Heroes. I had a meeting with the CEO, Bryn Parry, and his wife and co-founder, Emma. I had met Bryn Parry two years previously, interviewing him for an article I wrote for the *Mail on Sunday* about the-then fledgling charity. When I moved into the patch I had decided to be proactive and see if I could help in any way, by volunteering in the busy Tidworth office. Soon after arriving, Bryn had told me that their current head of media and PR had just handed in her notice (head sounds so grand, at this point the charity was tiny and the entire department consisted of just two people) and would I be interested in applying for the role? I drove home in a state of high excitement and of course applied. I got the job and my start date was the day Ed left for two months' training in Africa.

Kirsty, who had given up her job as a trainee reporter in Wales to move with Ben, also got a job with Help for Heroes and for all the efforts of the battalion, it was this that made her feel really at home in Tidworth. 'I became a working girl then and when you've got a group of girls your kind of age that you're working with it's a social life in itself,' she says. 'It's all I wanted – I came home to my husband and we wanted to spend all our time together and while he was busy, I was busy. They're lovely girls; Help for Heroes is frantically busy, but you can have a laugh on the way.'

Kirsty and I met in the Help for Heroes office, and within minutes we were sharing wedding photos and moving to the patch stories and within weeks, while Ben was away training, Kirsty was popping around for supper, my husband always insisting on walking her the five-minute journey home. Like Kirsty, I loved that I was making friends who were outside of my husband's regiment, yet who were also able to understand what being an army wife was all about. I enjoyed the ease of Help for Heroes, the relaxed nature of the relationships formed at work which meant you could be as involved or remote as you chose without anyone judging you (although the nature of the charity, and those who work for it, did tend to mean that the majority of staff would attend all events, mucking in willingly at weekends and in the evenings). This was unlike patch life which can, unwittingly, sometimes make you feel that if you don't join in, don't conform, other wives will think badly of you or even judge your husband. Help for Heroes wasn't like that and feels more like a family than any place I have ever worked before.

The community feel of patch life is something that is a source of great strength and comfort to army wives, and something that, as we will see later, comes into its own when your husband is away on tour. But living in such a close-knit community with your husband's colleagues and their families can have a flip side too, particularly in those moments when you're pining for the life you left behind.

Our houses all overlook one another and with the best will in the world it is impossible not to be nosey. You can clearly see all of your nearest neighbours' homes and it is obvious if someone has not drawn their curtains in the morning, or, judging by the cars outside, has not gone to work or has visitors. I remember one wife telling me how when she first moved to the patch, not working and child-free, she would often wear her PJs until lunch time, and stay in bed long after her husband left for work. Not wanting her neighbours to think her a sloven, she would jump up at a reasonable time and ensure that all the curtains in the house were drawn before sneaking back to bed, complete with eye mask, for a lie-in. That might sound a little over the top, but wives will text me to see if I am OK on the occasional days when I either forget or purposefully leave the curtains closed. Most of the time it is lovely to feel that people are watching out for you, but, as a Londoner, used to anonymity, it can also feel a little bit intrusive, as though nothing is private.

The closeness can also create a desire to conform and fit in, even it means doing things that are out of character. I still shudder at the memory of the time the regiment was having a bake sale in aid of a military charity, and one of the other wives asked me if I would make something. I said yes, of course, because my desire to fit in overruled the voice in my head reminding me that first, I had a really long day in the office ahead, and second, I was pretty hopeless at making cakes. Living in such a close community I felt that if I didn't, I would be letting the side down, and perhaps some of the other wives wouldn't like me.

As the clock ticked past 10 pm, I found myself still trying – and failing – to make cupcakes. The kitchen looked like a bomb had hit it – I had managed to get ingredients everywhere – even spilling flour on the poor dog, who had sensibly now taken refuge under the table. He peered up at me anxiously as if I had gone quite mad. Needless to say, the cupcakes were an unmitigated disaster and I ended up being too embarrassed to submit them. I was frustrated with the wives for asking me and myself for agreeing, but most of all with the feeling that I couldn't really have said no.

My lack of baking skills might not have won me any chocolate brownie points, but at least I didn't face a situation where my marriage itself made life a little awkward. One of the biggest shocks for Kirsty and Ben when they moved to the patch was realising that, in many ways, their marriage was disapproved of. It will seem old-fashioned to those outside of army life but a young officer is not encouraged to get married until he reaches the rank of captain. Even then, it is expected that he will write to his commanding officer to ask permission. To my knowledge, in recent history, this permission has never been denied but it is a tradition continued as a mark of respect and is a clear indication of how being a soldier is so much more than a nine-to-five job.

There is a good reason why the army prefers junior officers to wait before tying the knot. During the first few

years of being an officer, the men live together in the mess –
almost like going to a grown-up boarding school, where
they work, eat, drink and sleep under the same roof. There
are shared duties and a real sense of community, traditions
of the regiment are passed on and history remembered. It is
such a close-knit way of living that the men become more
than colleagues – a brotherhood between the men is forged,
and a sense of trust created that could prove crucial out on
the battlefield.

Those first few years of dinners together, of mess games,
arguments and banter are key to preserving the family nature
of a regiment. Ben, immediately living in married quarters,
would miss out on this rite of passage and – should the
other young officers feel he was getting special treatment,
shirking on duties because he lived out – the morale of the
officers' mess could be affected. As one of the most junior
officers, Ben found himself on duty frequently, working
weekends and evenings despite not living in. It was hard for
the young couple – they genuinely hadn't known the
convention of waiting to get married, and with a tour
looming, were desperate for as much of a married life as
possible before Ben went away. It seemed to Kirsty that Ben
was being forced to put the battalion before his wife and she
felt very resentful.

Against the backdrop of scenes of domesticity played out
in different houses across Tidworth, of dinner parties and
coffee mornings, cake sales and dog walks, is the underlying
dread of the next separation. Although a tour is officially six

months, long months of training beforehand means that, in reality, the best part of a year is taken up with one tour cycle. 'You start your pre-deployment cycle six months before you go away,' Ben explains, 'and you're constantly thinking, "I've got to maximise my time that I'm at home, because in two or four months' time I'm going to be in Afghanistan for six months." But you can't, because you are away training – weeks away, when I can't even call Kirsty, and working long hours when I am in Tidworth. It's intense – and then you're away for six months.'

As the men train, the wives go into a form of training themselves, a trial run of being alone, of missing their husbands. You can begin to dread a tour the minute you know that there will be one, even years before your husband is due to leave. My husband's regiment is due to go away in 2012 and although he will not be joining them I know wives who are already feeling sick at the thought. Sometimes there is much less notice – if someone is suddenly called upon to fill a role they can be give just a week to say their goodbyes. It is an endless topic of conversation amongst army wives – whether it is better to have time to gear up to your husband's departure, or have the separation just thrust upon you.

Veteran army wife Amanda likens it to the labour of childbirth – that you only remember how hard it is when you're experiencing it again. Despite having nine tours under her belt, she feels it has got harder as she has got older. 'A lot of younger wives look up to us and expect us to be strong because we've been there and done that,' she says. 'But as you get older you share a lot more with your partner, you want them around more so the separation is harder –

he's my soul mate and we're too long in the tooth to be apart. When you put it into context, the amount of time he's been away, it is quite a huge fraction of our entire life that we could have spent together. He's missed four years, in total, of our kids growing up.' She tells me, with a sigh, 'That's a quarter of our daughter's life that he's been away.'

In the early days of their marriage Lee 'only' went to Northern Ireland, but as the British Army committed its support in conflicts worldwide, Lee's absences from family life also increased. On some occasions there was only twelve months' respite before he was out on his next six-month tour. In one instance, Lee spent twelve months out of two years away, and that is not even taking into account the weeks of training exercises he took part in before he left.

For Rhiannon, she worried about her husband going to Afghanistan far more than she had dreaded any of his previous tours. The battalion had lost one soldier from the 2 R Welsh company already; he had been killed there six months previously to Huw deploying, so Rhiannon knew that her husband would face very real danger. 'People were dying by that point – we'd already had that happen,' she says. 'We all knew that there were more risks this time. There was the fact that Huw was now in this position of responsibility; going as an independent company, I knew that he would feel the pressure, that the buck stopped with him and he'd feel responsible for everybody – because he was. You had all the pressure – it was such an important job and he wanted to do well. He was so excited about it because it was basically what he'd joined the army to do – but we knew the risks and I was very worried.'

Rhiannon also had to deal with the fact that she was new to Tidworth. She hadn't had a chance to make many friends yet, and the girls living nearby were different wives from when she and Huw had been based with the battalion before. 'I was building up to it, the tour, getting used to him not being there when he was away training, making friends, and trying to keep busy – remembering how I used to fill the nights when he was away last time,' she explains. 'I was always OK, but if I came home from work Friday and didn't do anything until Monday, it was awful. I'd get to work on Monday and just gabble – not shut up for two hours, because I hadn't spoken to anybody. I knew I had to make a life for myself without Huw as quickly as possible. I was practising – I had three months to remember how you do it and cope with these things.'

Of the sixteen weeks leading up to deployment, Huw was away for twelve, because of training. And even for the weeks when he was at home, the description of what he'd been doing did little to calm Rhiannon's nerves. 'They did some riot training and the company went up and they had some other units playing the opposition,' she says. 'They actually had bombs going off, and fire – Huw came back from that training just in awe of the training. He had been so excited by it because it was so dangerous, so cutting edge, like you were really there. Concrete blocks were being chucked, people really going for it. He came back to me after that really fired up, and I was absolutely terrified.'

Longest-serving Daffodil Girl Simone hoped that this tour would be easier. Her sons were older and keen to look after mum and she thought that now, after nineteen years, it would be less painful. But in the weeks leading up to Mark's departure, Simone found that at times she couldn't even look at him without feeling like she was going to cry. 'I was shocked by how upset I was,' she says. 'Not that my love for him has changed, but I thought it would be easier; I just hate the build-up.'

There is no good time for the man you love to go away, but some times are more acutely painful than others. Army couples try desperately to plan their lives so the husband misses the least amount of important family moments, but, of course, things don't always work out like that. Life, as the saying goes, is what happens when you're making other plans.

Kirsty hadn't thought much of it when her period was a few weeks' late. She was fairly scatty about noticing when she was due at the best of times, and put it down to the stresses of moving and starting a new job. But when another week passed, even she thought it unusual, and decided to take a test. Kirsty and Ben had always planned to be young parents but even so, there was something about holding the pregnancy test in her hand that made Kirsty feel terrified. As she waited for the line to appear, she wasn't sure whether she feared or wanted the confirmation that she was going to be a mother.

Kirsty still wasn't convinced when the test came up positive, thinking it couldn't have been able to tell so soon. She sat there alone for a few moments, steeling herself before going into the living room to tell her husband. Ben, like Kirsty, didn't believe the result at first: he thought she must have got the instructions wrong. But when Kirsty did a second text, and that was positive, too, there was no doubting it. Somehow, none of it felt real to Kirsty, who felt a curious mixture of being thrilled and daunted at the same time. Ben, usually notoriously too hard to read, was clearly as excited as she was.

But if the news was wonderful, the timing was terrible. Ben was due to deploy in five months' time, and the baby would be due halfway through his tour. There was no escaping the fact that he would most likely miss the birth and definitely the first few months of their child's life. The looming tour, the first that Kirsty would experience, would have been difficult to cope with as it was. Now, though, their good news just made it even harder.

CHAPTER 4

'They're Soldiers, They'd Rather Be There In The Action'

Windswept and breathless, Amanda couldn't help but smile as she looked at the breathtaking views across the Snowdonia National Park. The family were in North Wales, enjoying some quality time together before Lee deployed for six months in Afghanistan; Lee – the adventurous one in the family – had decided to take his decidedly unsporty wife and two teenage daughters to climb to the top of Mount Snowdon. It had been a hard climb – over a thousand metres – and Amanda had complained on the way up, but now, husband and children by her side, she was so pleased she had been persuaded. Her cheeks flushed almost the same red as her Help for Heroes hoodie, Amanda couldn't help but feel really proud of herself as she posed for a photo – a photo to prove to friends she had done it, and to remind herself of happier times when Lee was away.

But if Amanda thought that tackling the highest peak in Wales was challenge enough, she was in for an even bigger surprise. A few days later and Lee had another more daunting activity planned for the family: Go Ape, a giant obstacle course high up in the trees, consisting of ladders, walkways, bridges and tunnels made of wood, rope and super-strong wire and zip lines. Kitted out with harnesses, the family were given a short safety briefing and training before being let loose into the forest canopy, free to swing through the trees.

There was just one small problem for Amanda to deal with – she is absolutely terrified of heights. Somehow, though, that didn't seem to be the most important issue. 'I did everything that he wanted to do,' says Amanda. 'Normally I would take it for granted that I could say "no", and I wouldn't do it. If he hadn't been going to Afghanistan, I wouldn't have done the Go Ape course in a million years but I actually didn't feel in a position to refuse. I wanted to know when he left for Afghanistan that I'd accommodated his wishes rather than do what I wanted. I wanted to make him happy before he went.'

Readying yourself for your loved one to leave for a war zone – something I did when Ed went to Iraq in 2007 – is a ghastly, gut-wrenching experience. From the date of deployment languishing in the comfort zone of being many months away, suddenly you're into weeks of wait and then, as if time is somehow speeding up, the days before their departure disappear so quickly that you can't keep up with them.

Separation, of course, is part and parcel of being an army wife. In the five years Ed and I have been together he has spent at least two months of each year solidly out of the country, and this is not including weeks away training in the UK. Each separation is painful and I have dreaded every single one. One of the worst for me was when, a few months into our marriage, Ed went to Africa for nine weeks. The build-up was terrible as I found myself resenting him for bringing me – and leaving me – in Tidworth. I would find myself switching between withdrawing, picking fights and getting angry, and being clinging, needy, wanting to touch him all the time and – like Amanda – spoil him as much as possible.

From the longer-serving Daffodil Girls, I'm a little relieved to learn that such behaviour is completely normal. 'You definitely do try to withdraw a little bit,' Simone tells me. 'I go up and down – some days I just want to sit next to him all the time, I want cuddles all the time. But on other days I find myself trying to distance myself. This time we did something we've never done before – we went on holiday a week before he went. I was dreading it, with him leaving, and wondered if it was going to spoil the holiday – but it was actually better. Although it was in the back of my mind all the time, the days were busy, and you weren't just sitting there thinking about it all the time as you normally are.'

Amanda tells me that when she and Lee were younger her attitude before he left was different. 'If he was going away we'd detach ourselves for about two weeks before he went, we'd pick and argue that little bit more,' she recalls. 'But this time there was none of that at all – totally different. I just

wanted to keep smelling him – be with him every second.'
Even, it seems, if that meant being attached to a harness,
halfway up a tree.

Every army couple has their own way of getting through
those fraught, final, precious weeks before deployment. For
some it is a time to squeeze the maximum enjoyment out of,
to go on holiday and treat themselves – partly to give themselves memories to treasure, partly to take their minds off
what is happening next. Others prefer the reassurance of
their regular routine, enjoying every last minute of everyday
life before the separation begins.

The usual pre-tour routine for Rhiannon and Huw would
be to go on holiday but this time, just before he left for
Afghanistan, they decided to stay closer to home. They went
to London for a week, had meals out and visits to the theatre
but the rest of the time they spent in their quarter in
Tidworth. As Rhiannon puts it, 'It wasn't romantic or
interesting. We would read the papers together, play stupid
computer games endlessly and watch telly. We're not very
swish with our hobbies. We'd sit for hours quietly, reading,
trying not to think about it. Our ninth wedding anniversary
was the day before he left, and we went out for dinner at a
local gastro pub, The Shears Inn. We had a nice dinner and
over the meal we talked and planned what we were going to
do this time the following year, post-tour, for our ten-year
anniversary.'

For Kaz and Brian the pre-tour time was not quite so
harmonious: there was friction between the couple. Kaz
wanted to do things, go out for a meal, go to the cinema,
spend what Kaz saw as quality time together before Brian left

but, she explained to me, her husband had different ideas. 'Brian likes to chill in the time before he goes away, literally do nothing. This is his house and he knows when he goes away how he will be living – with no home comforts. So he likes to stay in, chill out. It's difficult because I'm saying, "Let's go somewhere and do something because you're going to be away for three months." But he doesn't really want to, he just wants to sit on the sofa dressed in his *Rocky* dressing gown. It drives me crazy but,' she adds, echoing Amanda's comments, 'I let him do what he wants as he is the one who will be away from home. Not me.'

Donna didn't want to let Craig out of her sight – they had a lovely few weeks spending time together, making plans for their future and entertaining friends in their army quarter. But the weekend before Craig left, Donna sent him down to Wales alone. 'I knew that if Bradley and I went with him he'd be distracted and focused on us and I thought it was important for him to have quality time with his family – his mum and siblings and his mates,' she explains. 'Much as I wanted to be selfish with his time I knew I had to share him because other people loved my husband and were going to miss him too.'

When it was my turn, I found it impossible to be as generous with Ed's time. The first and only row I have had with his big sister was when I learned that she had arranged a surprise family party for Ed – to be held on the weekend before he left. 'He won't want that,' I insisted, 'he wants a quiet night with just us.' Emily is the granddaughter, daughter and niece of colonels (Ed's father retired just a few years ago and Ed is a fifth-generation soldier) and had also dated a soldier – she had far more experience of this than me at that time and knew that I was just upset about him leaving. Over the phone, while I tried to control indignant sobs, Emily gently reminded me that other people loved my boyfriend too – and had a right to say goodbye.

The evening was a great success but I must confess I still resented every second my man spent speaking to someone else – I really didn't want to share and found myself clinging to whatever part of him I could reach throughout the night – prompting his father to say 'Put him down, girl' as I stole another kiss. His tough military family must have thought I was a complete drip, but I couldn't help myself.

For Kirsty and Ben, meanwhile, the experience was a little more complicated: not only were the couple gearing up for Ben to go away, but they were also preparing for the arrival of their baby.

For Ben, knowing he would be away for the last stage of the pregnancy and then the first few months of the baby's life, finding out if he was going to have a daughter or son was a way to feel more involved and, he hoped, something that would bring him comfort when he was going through darker days in Afghanistan. The couple wanted to spend their last few weeks talking about names, being excited together and getting the nursery ready in a gender-appropriate colour. At the twenty-week scan, as the sonographer moved the transducer over her stomach, Kirsty clutched Ben's hand tightly not just because the jelly felt cold, but also because she was eager for Ben to know what sex the baby was going to be.

Kirsty wasn't as clingy as she thought she would be in the run-up to Ben going. That was probably due to being distracted by trying to get everything sorted for the baby while Ben was in the country, and making plans for post-tour, when their little family would be together for the first time. Ben had three weeks' leave before he left and the couple went away to Devon for four nights, staying in a small, idyllic cottage and walking their dog Lucy on deserted beaches. 'Really "old couple" holiday,' remembers Kirsty, 'but it was lovely.'

Back in Tidworth, the couple worked to make the smallest room in their house a nursery: a trip to IKEA provided a cot and nursing chair, which Ben put together while Kirsty, according to Ben, stood in the corner giving unhelpful advice. They painted an old chest of drawers of Ben's white to match the cot; Ben's auntie made bunting, which they strung across the walls and Kirsty's nan made curtains to match the walls that Ben was painting.

'Of course I felt really teary at times at the thought of him going,' says Kirsty, 'but it wouldn't be helpful to be crying all the time. Only Ben really knew how I was feeling and that was because I kept asking him ridiculous questions, making him make promises he couldn't keep – like that he would never go out on foot patrol, that he would always be safe. In my heart I knew he had no control over that but it made me feel better to hear him say it and of course doing up the nursery was a wonderful distraction.'

Back at the twenty-week scan, the baby wasn't playing ball in terms of revealing his or her gender. 'The way it was lying just meant that the sonographer couldn't tell,' Kirsty explains. 'It was a little bit frustrating but really, once we learned everything was looking fine, that was all that mattered – he/she being healthy was all we cared about.' The couple would just have to wait to find out what they were having, and hope the baby appreciated the nursery's freshly painted, gender-neutral, apple-green walls.

At some point in these last few weeks before deployment, every army couple has their version of 'The Conversation': the discussion that no wife wants to have, about what their husband would want, should the worst happen. It is a painful topic but one that army wives, new or old, are forced to have. Are the wills in orders? What would you want at your funeral service? No one wants to think about it, but when your partner is going somewhere where British soldiers are dying each week, you have to talk it through. As hard as the conversation might be, worse would be not being able to honour your partner in the way they would want.

When Ed went to Iraq, I really couldn't bring myself to talk about any of this. We were a relatively new couple and I didn't even want to be down as his next of kin: imagining being the one the bad news was told to was too much to bear. But a couple of years on, when I went to Afghanistan as a journalist to report from Kabul and Helmand, the Ministry of Defence strongly advised I made sure my wishes were known and I had an up-to-date will. So we sat down on the opposite sides of the table to have that talk. We had just got engaged and moved into our first home together, so it was fairly straightforward – everything would be Ed's. But there were small details, friends I would want him to look after, certain items I wanted to be given to loved ones – I put it all in my will, but we still had to talk it through. It was surreal and as the bottle of wine emptied we talked about what he would want as well – not monetary issues, but the rest. It is not a conversation many young couples are forced to have but for Ed and I, it was one which was important and necessary.

For Mandy and Ian, the moment to talk came in the early evening of a warm, sunny day. They were strolling hand in hand around the outside of the polo pitches, their dog Austin happily bounding alongside them. The pitches are one of the most beautiful parts of Tidworth, reached via a tree-filled area of parkland and standing behind one of the finest mansions in Wiltshire – Tedworth House. It is a favourite spot for dog walking in the area and, for Mandy and Ian, away from the children, the place they went to talk.

Ian took this moment to tell his wife that he wouldn't be writing a letter for her to be given to her in the event of his death. Many soldiers do this and, in some regiments, are advised too by the commanding officer – the idea being that it would be some small comfort to the partner left behind. But Mandy understood her husband's reasons completely. 'I didn't want him to have to write that, thinking he might not come home. We know how we feel about one another and I didn't need a letter to tell me how he felt about me and the kids – I know how much he loves us.'

The bathroom always seemed to be the place where Kaz and Brian would talk about the serious stuff. A week before

Brian left for Afghanistan, lying in the bath with a beer in hand, he told his wife in detail what he would want at his funeral. Kaz was shocked and realised that her young husband really thought he might not come home. 'He knew how dangerous it was out there,' remembers Kaz, 'and he was scared.' Painful though the conversation was, Kaz was glad they had had it, glad that she now knows what he would want if, God forbid, something did happen to him, that she could carry out his wishes. 'It's not nice to have to talk about it but I think it's something you have to do, especially when they go away,' she says.

With Pete's deployment a week away, Elaine and Pete also felt they should have the conversation. Once the children were in bed, they sat down in the sitting room, their dog Buster lying between them. They covered everything: the flowers he'd like, what he would want to wear, the songs he would want played. 'It's horrible,' says Elaine, 'but if I know what he wants then I'd know it would be perfect. I don't get upset, because I know if I do, he will too and he won't want to go. It is so sad to even think about anything happening to Pete but if it did, I know I'd feel a lot better knowing he got what he wanted, rather than me giving him what I think he'd like.'

Donna and Craig really didn't want to have the conversation. Both in their early twenties, it seemed unimaginable that anything could happen to him. But, at a welfare briefing in camp, they were advised to talk things through as well as to make sure the welfare office had full contact details for Donna – and for her to tell them if she was going away so that if something were to happen, they would be able to find her.

After the briefing Craig forced himself to tell his young wife where he would want his ashes to be scattered and the name of a friend he would want to sing at his funeral, but that was it – as far as either of them wanted to go.

Instead of focusing on the unimaginable, the couple talked about plans for when he did come home, plans for their future. The first thing Craig said he wanted to do was officially adopt Bradley: Craig was the only man the three-year-old had ever called daddy and Craig was anxious to make the boy legally his son. The couple wanted to save the bonus money Craig would get while away on tour to put towards a deposit for a home in the town in Wales where Craig grew up – where they eventually wanted to live and raise a family. 'It was better that way,' says Donna, 'making happy plans for the future rather than thinking about the worst-case scenario we were both happier that way.'

Amanda found herself unable to stop endlessly asking Lee what he would want if something did happen to him, checking that his will and insurance were in order. In reality, she already knew the answer to the questions she kept asking but, asking those questions was a way to let him know how scared she was without having to say the words. 'I couldn't help it,' says Amanda. 'I'd say to Lee, "Don't go running around – you're not a young boy any more. You're a forty-one-year-old man and your knees click when you stand." I don't want him to be a glory-seeker, I just want him to do his job, for the time to be over quickly and him to come back safe. He realised how scared I was, kept reassuring me that he'd being doing what he's trained to do, but that didn't make it any easier or make me any less worried.'

For Rhiannon and Huw, the conversation happened at odd moments, as opposed to a planned discussion. 'You don't think, "Now let's sit at the kitchen table and we'll have this conversation,"' Rhiannon explains. 'Suddenly you might be driving somewhere and you hear something on the radio about wills. Then you think, "Oh, have we got to do that?" It would usually be the most inappropriate time to start talking about it. It was always random and we'd just get chatting. That's what I'm like. Then Huw might just say, "Let's not talk about this anymore." He would generally be the one to say, "I'm done now," whether it was because he was upset or bored.'

Rhiannon tended to be the one to initiate the topic. 'It always came from me,' she says. For her, it was more of a practical than an emotional matter. 'I sat down to make sure all the life insurance was there and the illness cover . . . I wanted to get our wills up to date. Huw didn't really like to talk about the practical side of things – but I needed to get all my ducks in a row. We talked about that more than how we would feel if something happened to him.'

Dereynn and Taff only found it possible to talk about the unthinkable when they were out seeing another Daffodil Girl and her husband. 'We were sitting with Julie and Dai, and we got on to the subject of funerals – what Taff and Dai would want,' Dereynn explains. The fact that they were talking with friends somehow made the subject more approachable for her. 'The chat with Julie and Dai, it wasn't a husband and wife thing and I felt at ease because I was doing it with friends – I wouldn't have asked if I'd been at home.'

Out of all the tours Taff had been on, this was the first time Dereynn had approached the subject. 'I'd never asked him – because that's me saying to myself he's going to go away and something's going to happen. But this time it's Afghanistan.'

At the back of Dereynn's mind was what nearly happened to Taff in Iraq. He was due to come home on leave on the Tuesday, but because the then newly appointed prime minister, Gordon Brown, was flying in for a visit, the dates were changed and Taff flew back a day early. 'He came home on the Monday and on the Wednesday we were in camp when someone came up to us and asked if we'd heard the news. It turned out that the area he had slept in and worked from had been bombed. I just sat there – thinking, "Oh my God." He'd come home on the Monday and that happened on the Tuesday.'

Dereynn feels her attitude to what might happen is different to some of the other Daffodil Girls. 'You hear many of the wives saying that if anything happens, they've done it for the job they love doing, and that's always one thing I've never said to hubby. I just don't like to say "If anything happens to you, how would you like to go?" To me that's like saying, "ta-ra", and I don't like saying that – I like to have him to come home to me.'

Mandy lay on the bed and watched her husband pack. He wasn't very organised, keeping a list in his head and just shoving everything in his bag as he went – frequently asking his wife if he had indeed just packed a particular item. It is his habit to always sort out his work kit at work, in fact the only time Mandy ever sees his army greens or combat uniform is when it need washing. Ian is meticulous that it should all remain in his locker and changes out of his civvies each morning when he gets to work, similarly changing to come home again.

As he packed, the couple talked normally – Ian about how he was gutted to be missing the rugby. He referees in his spare time and as Mandy explains, 'He's got a different love for us than he has for rugby. He misses that as much as he does us, I suppose. It's a big passion in his life – I was teasing him because he was going to miss the season.'

Mandy and Ian talked about how they would stay in touch – Ian asked Mandy to encourage their two children to write as often as possible, and said in turn that he would be in touch as much as he was able. Mandy didn't help him pack and didn't get upset as she watched him. 'For us, at that point,' she says, 'it is just a case of let's get it on and get it started. We try to work on the basis that the sooner we get it started, the sooner it's finished, and he's coming back.'

The packing of the kitbag is the moment when the waiting is over, and the countdown to deployment has begun. It might not sound much, but it carries a powerful emotional punch for both husband and wife, a small but symbolic ritual that each soldier enacts in his own particular way. Not every army wife is blessed with the cool composure that Mandy has: whenever Ed packs, I tend to have to leave the room.

Ed's routine is meticulous. He begins by laying out everything first, to ensure he has all of his kit, before beginning the job of packing it away. Like a petulant child I find myself desperate to remove each item as he puts it in his bag and fling it across the room as if that somehow will stop him from leaving. So, once I have slipped a love letter and perhaps a photograph into his bag, it is easier for both of us if I sit downstairs, nursing a glass of wine, until he is finished.

Mark didn't like Simone to watch him pack, knowing that more often than not his wife would end up in floods of tears. So he put the moment off for as long as he could, and then he would try to sneak away when he knew she was busy with something else. Like Ed, Mark packs with military precision, making sure that he has everything – all laid out in front of him – before he starts to put it away.

He wasn't looking forward to going away, but Mark had admitted to Simone that he did want to go to Afghanistan. It is a big part of our modern military history and Mark knew he wanted to take part in it. Despite her dread at him leaving, Simone did understand. 'They're soldiers, and as hard as it is for them to go and leave all their home comforts, they would rather be there in the action than stuck back here in camp, hearing about what's going on over there,' she says. 'Mark is coming to the end of his career now and if he had finished without ever going to Afghanistan it would have felt incomplete to him somehow.'

Ben took only two days to complete his packing and, according to Kirsty, that was pretty organised, for him. He decided to pack in their living room, and gradually the normally tidy room became filled with his clutter. Ben was taking what seemed to be a bewildering array of kit: because he was going to be deployed for both the summer and winter he needed clothing that could cope with all temperature extremes, from freezing cold to boiling hot. The warm hat with ear-flaps entertained Kirsty – 'Ben really can't carry off hats' – and all the safety equipment, which Ben went to great lengths to show his wife, reassured her. She wanted to help so busied herself finding plastic boxes for his toiletries. Although she tried not to show it, she felt more and more upset as each item disappeared into her husband's bag.

Bradley was asleep, so Donna was able to lie on the bed and talk to Craig as he packed. Dressed casually in tracksuit bottoms and a T-shirt, Craig wasn't too organised when it came to packing and was hopeless at finding everything. He also wasn't very tidy, so packing was a long process, with him having to pause frequently to seek out the next item. The fact that he had no list also meant he was distracted, trying to remember everything he needed to take with him. Once he had everything he needed, however, he made sure it was put in his kitbag very neatly.

Donna was feeling OK about him leaving, 'It was odd – you know that they're going and you've only got limited time so feel as though everything you say and do should be important, but here we were, me watching him pack talking about nothing in particular. I wasn't even dreading saying goodbye – or the first week – I was looking forward to my house being clean all the time.' She pauses, 'But I knew that once the week was over I'd just want him home.'

PART TWO

THE TOUR

CHAPTER 1

'The Weekends Are The Worst.
The House Is Tidy – No Rugby, No Boxing'

The first thing that Dereynn does after saying goodbye to her husband Taff, apart from having a good cry, is to clean the house from top to bottom, putting away every trace of her husband. She strips their bed, putting on fresh sheets and does the washing that he will have inevitably left in the wash basket. His trainers get put out of sight and any bits of army kit left lying around are cleared away, taking him out of their home until he returns. She does, in her own words, 'remove every trace' of her husband, bar one thing; normally a T-shirt or perhaps his pillowcase, something that smells of Taff so when she has a down day, feels she has had enough, she can inhale deeply and be comforted by the familiar smell of the man she loves.

For Kirsty, tidying was also high on the agenda – the

house had turned into a complete tip while she dedicated all of her spare time to Ben, doing all the things he wanted to do before he left and spending as much time together as possible. But now, with him gone, she wanted to make their home lovely again in the hope that doing so would distract her from how much she was already missing him. Kirsty also had another concern – in the days and weeks before Ben left she had plagued her young husband with constant anxious questions about the tour, often being negative, and she knew that he had left for Afghanistan upset and worried about his wife. 'I wish I'd been a bit more calm,' Kirsty says 'but I'm rubbish in terms of army wife-ing. I keep forgetting that this whole me being left pregnant is hard on him too. He feels guilty about leaving me, probably.' Just an hour after dropping Ben in camp Kirsty texted him, hoping to reassure him. 'I love you so much,' she wrote. 'Don't worry about me. I'll be OK with my Lucy-dog. Had a lovely greeting from her when I got home. Hopefully speak to you before you fly. Take care, gorgeous.' And then she felt a bit better, hopeful that now she had played her role as army wife as best she could and Ben knew she supported him. Then, despite the best intentions, she collapsed on to the blue army-issue sofa and cried into the fur of Lucy, the couple's beloved Border Terrier.

Kaz, meanwhile, goes one better than just cleaning the house: she responds to Brian's departures by deciding to redecorate. She was determined that within days of her husband leaving she would have transformed their army quarter sitting room. It had been the same for eighteen months now and she was ready for a change, the blue curtains, pillows and other touches feeling a little chilly for the upcoming winter months, especially as she would be spending them alone. Kaz wanted a warmer look and redecorating would keep her busy for the first and, Kaz felt, the toughest week Brian was away.

A few days later and she was finished, the sofa was moved to the other side of the room, its neutral colour the perfect backdrop for scatter cushions in vibrant purples and calm lilacs. The new rug was down – the purple rug perfectly offsetting the new curtains, which Kaz had hung by herself, balancing precariously on a stepladder. Kaz was really pleased with how it looked but, even more important, thrilled that the transformation had made the first few days of the tour go as quickly as possible. Redecorating has become a bit of a tradition for Kaz, and Brian always knows when he comes home, he's coming home to a different house. 'It makes it lovely for when he comes back,' Kaz says, 'shows him that I haven't just been sitting around – that I've been doing something, making the home nicer for us.'

Every army wife has developed her own coping mechanism for dealing with the departure of her husband: tried, tested and perfected after years of goodbyes. For after the emotional farewell, there is a life that every wife has to get on with. Figuring out how to live on your own is probably the most important, and the hardest, thing for a new army wife to learn. When Ed went away for two months, after just three months' marriage, I came home from work, lay on the living-room floor and sobbed while our young puppy pawed me anxiously – those first few days are always the hardest, knowing there are months to go .

For Simone, the realisation that Mark had gone didn't really sink in until a couple of days after he'd left. 'It suddenly hit me like a ton of bricks, maybe because it was the weekend; I was really low and couldn't stop crying,' she recalls. By some strange quirk of fate, the day realisation hit for Simone was also the day that Mark finally got to Afghanistan, – a sandstorm in Camp Bastion, Helmand, meant that his plane was unable to land and they had been delayed. Exhausted after three days of travelling, the first thing Mark did was to find a phone and call his wife. 'It was so lovely to hear from him,' Simone says. 'I was at home not really expecting a call but when the landline rang I knew it was him, as he is the only person who has the number. We had a brief chat and for both of us the tour began at that moment – as soon as they're there, and they've settled, and you hear their voice, you can start thinking, "Right, now I've got to get into a routine, I've got to survive this."'

That feeling of needing to survive, to get through the tour, is one that is felt by most army wives, that despite being safe at home this is your tour too. Probably the worst year of my life was when Ed went to Iraq – as bad luck would have it, my best friend's (and flatmate's) boyfriend was deploying to Afghanistan the week Ed was coming home. It was a tough year – the first half spent with me in tears, missing Ed, desperate for a phone call or a letter while Cara and Tom (a newer couple) spent as much time as possible together and began to dread his tour. When Ed came home it was Tom's turn and although I tried my hardest to support my best friend, pained to witness her going through what I had, I was also desperate to just be with Ed. Then, Cara and I living together was almost like a practice run for living on the patch, having in close proximity another woman who really understood what you were going through. We helped each other as best we could while also ensuring our boys got as much time with us as possible. Cara and I are not sure that a day went by that dreadful year without one of us calling the other in tears. Like me, Cara had never planned to fall in love with an army officer but once Ed and I got serious and she started coming to various dinner nights and balls as our guest it was almost inevitable that she would. I didn't like the thought of Cara going through the trials and tribulations of being an army girlfriend but it was clear Tom was crazy about her and made her happy, despite the separations. They are to be married later this year and I am now thrilled to have one of my oldest and best friends as a fellow army wife.

After that first tour I thought nothing could be as hard again but now – a few years on and after talking to the older Daffodil Girls – I realise how wrong I was, and how much harder it will be if Ed is sent away when we have children. 'I do feel it's my tour of duty as well,' Dereynn says. 'They go away but we're the ones on tour here because we have to become mum and dad, nursemaid and bottle-washer. You have to do everything on your own and it is like being a single mum. I used to feel it wasn't fair, that he was swanning off for six months playing soldier while I was left behind with two kids. The first tour was a really big adjustment. I was used to him being away four weeks, or six weeks – but six months, that's six months out of our lives. He missed so much and for some reason always seems to miss Sian's birthday. It's easier now the kids are older, grown-ups really, because they understand but it was hard to explain to a little girl that daddy did still care, even though he was missing her birthday.'

Amanda echoes Dereynn, 'The person left behind looking after the kids is mother, father – they do absolutely everything. It's a big responsibility, especially for young wives with young kids.' But despite her children being older now, Amanda finds tours harder than ever before. Married for eighteen years, she and Lee have become much more dependent on each other. 'As you get older you depend on each other a lot more and there's more companionship there, you can only really experience it when you've been with someone a long time – your relationship goes on to a different level,' she says. 'It's strange, but it's comfortable as well – you become comfortable with each other and if that's taken away, it changes everything.'

I had naively (and maybe hopefully) imagined that for Amanda, Dereynn, Simone, Mandy and Julie, the longest-serving Daffodil Girls, older and wiser than me, a tour wouldn't be as hard, that they would be used to it. Speaking to each of them, this is clearly not the case. Amanda says, 'The first two days after Lee left I spent curled up on the sofa in my pyjamas, curtains closed, crying sporadically and I still have days now, a few weeks in, when I spend the whole day in tears, yet this is our ninth tour.'

*

The flashpoints of loneliness happen at different times for different Daffodil Girls. For several, last thing at night is when it really hits home that their husband isn't there. Dereynn, for example, always puts a brave face on it, laughing and joking with friends that she is glad Taff has gone away because now she can sleep in a star shape in the marital bed. But the reality is Dereynn finds it much harder to relax – to sleep easy, without the reassuring bulk of her husband, his steady breathing, helping her drop off – far more than she would ever like to admit.

Dereynn is not the kind of woman you would imagine scaring easily and yet, when husband Taff is away, she gets into a nightly ritual of locking every door and window and checking each lock before bed. When her son is out at work she hates the oppressive silence at teatime, finding herself looking at the door expectantly, as if Taff might walk in at any minute when the reality is that this is just the start of the tour and she know he's not coming home for months yet.

The first few weeks are the hardest. After that, Dereynn starts to get used to being on her own but, she says, 'I don't like it because he's not there. I can be brave in the house but when my youngest did night shifts, heading out to work as I went to bed, leaving me alone in the house, that was nerve-racking, it was horrible – you think about someone trying to get in – you make sure all the doors are locked. You hear a noise and you wonder what it is.'

Dereynn is not the only wife to get scared on her own – Tidworth feels by far the safest place in which I have ever lived, but when Ed was away I found myself checking and double-checking that I had locked the back door at bedtime – locking myself in as soon as I got home. The dog was a huge comfort (and of course, within days of Ed's departure was happily ensconced in our room at bedtime despite Ed and I agreeing that dogs are downstairs pets) but at night the creaks and groans of our old army house would send my imagination into overdrive. I had never lived in such a big house on my own and the yawning blackness of the two spare rooms would make me run back to my bed, heart thudding, after a visit to the loo in the middle of the night.

I am not alone in this – even the most independent of women can be spooked by an empty house when their husband is in a war zone. Kaz remembers the tour before this one, when Brian was away and her daughter (from her first marriage) was away at boarding school, 'Every noise had me jumping out of bed, grabbing the Samurai sword that he keeps on the windowsill just in case we had a burglar. I must have looked insane in my stripped PJs brandishing a ridiculous sword. Of course I wouldn't have known what to do if someone actually had broken in, but having the sword made me feel better.'

For other Daffodil Girls, it is getting through the weekend that proves particularly difficult. Simone sums it up, 'Everybody gets ready to spend the weekend with their husbands – and when everybody's not in the same position as you, you feel lonely – and that's the hardest part.'

While across the country the majority of people count down the days and then the hours until Friday night arrives, some army wives watch the clock ticking down with opposite emotions. 'The weekends are the worst,' says Kaz, 'because when they're in work in the week he comes home for lunch and goes back, and a lot of the time they're away training. But it's the weekends I find difficult – getting up in the morning and there's no Brian. The house is tidy – no rugby, no boxing. No *Rocky* dressing gown. I hate Sundays – and Sunday afternoon is bottle-of-wine afternoon to chill out, then I usually have an early night.'

The alternative to staying home at the weekend is also difficult for some wives: it can feel strange to go out and enjoy yourself when you know what your husband is up against. 'I don't like going out and having lots of fun when he's away,' Simone says. 'A lot of wives think differently and their attitude is that you still have to get on with your life, and that's true, but even after all these years, I've still got that little bit inside me that feels guilty if I have a bit of fun: he's stuck over there, doing that job he's doing, and I shouldn't be having fun. Even though I haven't got the type of husband who would begrudge me, you still feel it.'

That is a sentiment Kaz knows only too well. I always feel guilty going out, even though Brian would say "Go". Because I'd think, "I'm sitting here, enjoying myself, laughing, with a glass of wine, and he's lying in some ditch somewhere with all his body armour on, waiting for the next bullet to be fired." It is difficult. But always, if he phones home, I'll say, "The girls have asked me to go out,"' and he'll say, "You go, have a nice time." But I only went out once during the six-month tour, other than getting together with the girls in houses.'

For Ed's tour I was lucky to have fellow army girlfriends in the same boat to get me through the weekends. The first weekend (which was a bank holiday so even longer to fill) my friend Jess and I drank more than could possibly have been healthy and slept fitfully side by side in Jess's double bed, both wearing a T-shirt belonging to our boyfriends, before spending the Sunday drinking Bloody Marys and trying not to cry. When Ed went away more recently I drove to my mum's most weekends – moping around the house and, totally unfairly, seething with resentment at my brother and his girlfriend for going about their happy life together. The mantra is always to keep busy but after a hectic working week it can be exhausting trying to find someone to spend time with, and keeping positive in front of friends and family when really all you want to do is cry – or have your husband back.

Life, though, doesn't just stop while your husband is away. 'The first week was pretty difficult,' says Kaz, 'as is usually the case when they go away.' But after that, she started to pick herself up and make the effort to get out more. 'I've just been down to Wales to visit family – which was lovely. Great to see them and I stayed with my mother for three days and she spoiled me rotten – I could have stayed another week. You just have to say to yourself, "Come on, you've got to get on with it now – you can't be sitting in your house miserable for six months. You're no good to anybody." And you do that – you fill your time, finding things to do, and you just get on with it.'

Simone found herself facing such a situation as soon as Mark left: the day of his departure was her birthday. Simone wanted to run outside, follow Mark and shout 'Don't go – please don't go!' 'I know it sounds melodramatic – but that's how I feel when he first goes,' she explains. 'I think, "Come back!", as if it's my last chance to speak to him. It was such a horrible day because it was my birthday. It sounds silly, but that brought it home to me, how lonely it would be without him. Even though I'd do anything to have him home now, I'm so glad that that day's gone – the first day is just terrible. Every time you do it, it's like déjà vu, as if there hasn't been any gap in between the tours. You start thinking, "I can't believe I'm doing this again." It physically hurts.'

Simone knew that being kept busy was far better than sitting at home alone, so she went to work as normal. That night, Simone didn't feel in the mood for celebrating; she didn't want to do anything, or see anyone. But her son Dale and his girlfriend had other ideas, finally persuading Simone to come out with them for supper at the local Pizza Hut – Simone's favourite restaurant. 'They're an absolute rock in times like this,' Simone says. 'It's easier now Dale is older – he can look after me, rather than the other way round.'

The coincidence of Simone's birthday and Mark's departure is nothing unusual: it is typical of army timings that if there is a wedding, an important birthday or even a funeral, you can bet anything that something will happen to ensure your soldier misses the day. I have gone to so many weddings, engagement parties, and other events without Ed that I got into the habit of calling him my 'imaginary boyfriend' (now husband) telling friends 'he is real – I promise' and joking that I should get a life-size cut-out photo of him to take with me.

Kirsty, too, had got used to being the only 'attached-yet-single' person at parties while Ben was away, first as Sandhurst then later when he was training before Afghanistan. But, even with that practice, nothing was quite as frustrating, and lonely, as the first weekend after Ben left for Afghanistan. The couple had a wedding to attend, the first of their friends to get married and one of Ben's best friends – he was going to be an usher and both were looking forward to the day. Ben was due to fly to Afghanistan the following Monday, so they were just going to make it and Kirsty had had her favourite Coast dress, which has a flattering A-line style (which fitted over her bump) with cream and white stripes, dry cleaned in preparation. But of course nothing goes according to plan when you are married to a soldier. Ben's flights were brought forward, leaving Kirsty in a quandary – the last thing she wanted to do was go to a wedding alone, just days after saying goodbye to Ben, but she already felt bad that the couple had been let down by Ben's absence, leaving them minus an usher at such short notice. She came to a compromise – she would go to the service, then sneak off before the reception. It wasn't a sit-down do and she felt sure everyone would understand.

The morning of the wedding Kirsty was running late. She hadn't worked out the route and the last seven months of living with Ben had made her lazy, used to her officer husband taking charge of all navigating. She called one of Ben's friends who gave her directions but with no one in the passenger seat to help and a couple of wrong turns, Kirsty found herself fifteen minutes late, standing outside the church, its big heavy door very firmly shut.

'I sat outside, all dressed up, until they came out,' says Kirsty. 'The bride and groom saw me immediately but I don't think they minded and then I blended in with the rest of the guests and I don't think anybody else noticed; I snuck off as soon as I had stayed enough time to be polite. They only know me as Ben's wife and they're his friends and not necessarily mine – they're lovely guys, but I wouldn't have felt comfortable, sober, trying to mingle all night on my own. I am sure they all understood that it would be hard going for me, no matter how nice everyone is to you. Weddings are rubbish to go to solo – especially when your husband is in a war zone.'

This was something I could identify with – three years previously, one of my dearest friends walked down the aisle as my distressed sobbing distracted the whole congregation. Ed was in Iraq and that day three soldiers had been killed – I knew he was OK but the realisation that he had been nearby, plus his absence from my side on this most important of days, left me an emotional wreck. Most of the people there (I hope) assumed I was crying with happiness on the bride's wedding day, but she and her father knew that there was more to it than that and as they passed me he patted my back reassuringly – while she turned and gave me the most loving of smiles.

Despite the loneliness of the first few weekends there is something every army wife can be sure of – that somewhere on the patch there is someone in the same boat as you and that there are people just beyond the front door who will help you if you only ask. Sian is a younger Daffodil Girl, daughter to Dereynn and Taff, she has been brought up in the battalion, arriving in Hong Kong aged just three and now, aged twenty-four, married to a soldier (from a different battalion) and living just a short drive from her parents' home in her own army quarter. Sian has lived the life of army daughter and now wife and she wouldn't have it any other way. 'I love the sense of family – I have my family, but my family's also out there, in every other house,' she says. 'I have brothers and sisters all round, because we're a family battalion. I have other mums, people I can go to and say, "I've got an issue I can't talk to my mum about – I need to talk to you." I know I have that out there – it's amazing support from everywhere. You go to the shop and say, "Hi – haven't seen you in a while, I've got a problem," and they'll just drop everything to help. You wouldn't get that outside the army.

'To a new wife on the patch, I'd say, "Don't be afraid to ask for help when needed," because you'll get all the help you need from army wives. If you're out of sugar, knock on your neighbour's door – and she'll give you sugar and say, "Have some teabags as well," because you're all in the same boat, no matter what. We're a unit, background and rank don't matter – certainly it's never mattered in my dad's battalion. You're all the same when you're army wives, you're no rank – you're a "wife of". Some army wives don't understand that and are a bit hesitant to befriend army wives of higher ranks; they think rank is an issue for wives but it's not like that at all – nothing could be further from the truth.'

From daughter of the battalion (and now new army wife) up to the longest-serving 2 R Welsh wife, enjoying the sense of community on the patch goes across the board and it really comes into its own when the men go away. When Ed went away that freezing January I enrolled Freddie in paid 'puppy day care' (the dog normally went to work with Ed or stayed at home with me, but the start of my new job at Help for Heroes coincided with Ed's time away, meaning we had to find help to look after him). But within days it was clear it wasn't working – I was adjusting to my new job and a long commute, so never managed to pick him up when I said I would. The person having him became frustrated and we both agreed I should find somewhere else for him to go. When I got home that night I posted a jokey Facebook status: 'Expelled from puppy day care – oh the shame.'

I didn't expect any response, and the post was really for the benefit of my naughty London friends who I knew would find it entertaining, but within hours three wives had got in touch to offer to look after the dog. One of them, Sarah, who I had met only once before, even went as far as to collect him (despite living off the patch, twenty minutes away) and invite me to stay for supper and the night so I could be 'looked after and spoilt for an evening'. Georgia, the daughter of a colonel from my husband's regiment, at home while she applied for drama school, started to collect Freddie daily, always inviting me for wine and food when I came to pick him up quite late. Those glasses of wine, drunk in front of a roaring fire with Georgia and her parents, kept me going through the first scary month of a new job, new home and Ed being away. Then, when Georgia left, Jess stepped in; despite having a young baby and (she won't mind me saying this) a slightly crazy dog of her own, she welcomed having Freddie – helping me more than she'll ever know. I'll never forget arriving at her gate to find her with rubber gloves on, rubbing both the dogs down with ketchup before hosing them off, 'Best way to get off fox poo – they've both been rolling in it,' she explained. 'No, don't help and get mucky – you go and put the kettle on.' I have best friends who wouldn't go that far in the name of friendship, so to have a neighbour to do so was nothing short of amazing.

All these wives went out of their way to help and support me and in doing so taught me an important lesson about being an army wife. Amanda explains it best, 'Your friendships in this scenario are different – you depend on friendship a lot more and you're there for each other more. You build a good community spirit – it takes you back about forty years – in that you've got an old-fashioned sense of community where people are happy to help out and look after other people's children when they have a doctor's appointment, etc. It's better because it's a usually a group of wives who are all going through the same thing. They know how it feels to be supported from one side, and you reciprocate that by helping out the people who help you – and those that haven't necessarily, but might in the future. It has a knock-on effect and you help yourself by helping others.'

CHAPTER 2

'The Force Behind The Forces'

Most of the regimental DIY nights were a bit messy, but the night the wives tackled plastering was complete, yet wonderful, shambolic chaos. Captain Mo, welfare officer of 2 R Welsh, had arranged for an outbuilding in the back yard of the welfare house to be used by a group of wives, whose husbands were deployed in Afghanistan, to learn how to plaster and skim walls, and then tile and paint. Mo had managed to beg or borrow plastering gear; the material to make the plaster, the mixer drill, buckets, plaster boards, even boiler suits, for each of the wives with their names written on the back; some using their first names or, as their husband would have on his uniform, just their surnames. Captain Mo had everything covered – including a supply of wine.

That night there were about twelve women attending. They started arriving from about six onward, some a bit shy at first but the children (around twenty, of varying ages) soon broke the ice, running around with one another; littlies being looked after by the older ones. After a brief introduction by Mo, the women split into two teams; half to be outside cracking on DIYing in the outbuilding, while the other half stayed inside, catching up with one another – glass of wine in one hand and normally a child in the other. Mo talked the first group of girls through how to plaster – putting the drill in the bucket and mixing the plaster and water. Then he went into the outbuilding, first with a spatula to show them how it was done – smoothing out the plaster and working it gradually across the wall. 'Do it slowly,' he advised the group of women who were only half-listening, instead giggling to one another as they fondly renamed the welfare officer Bob the Builder because he was wearing (rather proudly it must be admitted) a belt round his waist filled with tools, most of which he obviously didn't need for plastering.

Then it was the wives' turn: Mandy volunteered to go first, her husband was company sergeant major for the men deployed to Afghanistan and she played as active a role as possible in all welfare events. But her first attempt at plastering did not go according to plan. 'I went far too fast with the drill and there was plaster powder going everywhere. Mo was shouting, "Don't do that, it can burn you." But I couldn't seem to make it slow down – everyone was laughing.'

The atmosphere was wonderful that evening – although some of the wives were meeting for only the first or second time, the activity was a great ice-breaker. Most of the women enjoyed a glass of wine or more, for with so many hands to look after the children, this was as close to a night off as many of the army mothers would get that week; and for those with no children, a small hangover at work the next day seemed a fair price to pay for a fun evening. Slowly, Mo's carefully-planned evening descended into pandemonium. Wives were plastering with one hand, smoking a cigarette with the other, children were in and out of the shed and welfare office trailing plaster dust with them as they went; a couple of the older ones had pulled on spare boiler suits, sleeves and trouser legs trailing, they looked like mini *Ghostbusters*. The first group of wives were weak with merriment after watching one another's attempts at plastering and, as they handed the shed over to the second team of women, the children decided they wanted a go: around eighteen pairs of grubby mitts were straight into the bucket and they began plastering everywhere, including each other– some of the little ones ending up covered in plaster from top to toe.

The night went on till past ten when eventually Mo had to kick out the last few remaining wives – the shed was a mess, but the evening had been a fantastic success. 'It was just one night when we could release a bit and chill out with other people who were feeling the same as us,' explains Mandy. 'A few hours of letting our hair down, with the kids happy playing with other children.'

There is an organised system within every battalion or regiment to try and ensure that while the men are on tour the battalion family looks after the wives and children. Welfare officer is one of the toughest jobs in a battalion, usually taken on by an LE (late entry) officer, a captain who because he has worked his way up through the ranks, knows what it is like for everyone – from the most junior private to the more senior officer. They are never off-duty and will answer phone calls late into the night – often to the chagrin of a long-suffering wife. Even when there aren't men deployed, it is still a full-time role with the welfare officer there to advise and help soldiers and their families, from giving financial advice to organising a quiz night.

The welfare officer is an intricate part of the morale and well-being of the battalion family. Mo, welfare officer for 2 R Welsh for just under two years now, has taken the job far above and beyond the call of duty. Rhiannon, whose husband Major Huw commanded A Company in Afghanistan, explains, 'The welfare office came into its own this tour, more than any other one I have been involved in. Mo was relentless, in a fabulous way – if a wife wasn't going to a DIY night, or coffee morning or weekend activity, it wasn't because Mo hadn't asked you to come along, personally. There's a difficulty sometimes, especially if you are new or young – you'll get a note through the door "We're all meeting on Wednesday night" and it takes quite a brave person to just turn up on their own, but Mo literally went to every wife and knocked on their door to invite them. Of course some people weren't interested, but I do hope that there was no one, despite everyone's best efforts, who was still too shy to come. The DIY was the funniest thing, regimentally, that I've ever done – we started in the summer and everyone was happy to be outside but when we got to November it was freezing and the project never quite got finished. We did plastering, tiling, beading, painting – a whole project to get this ridiculous outhouse up to scratch. But it was never really about that – just people hanging out and talking and having somewhere to go and knowing that one night that week there was fun to be had if you wanted to be there.'

As well as DIY, Mo also organises mechanics lessons, wine tasting and flower-arranging nights, weekend trips and a weekly coffee morning. Unfazed by hiccups such as the florist cancelling or not being a wine expert, without fail the welfare officer rolls up his sleeves and makes sure every night is a success.

'For wine tasting he'd get a DVD or a book explaining how to do a wine tasting,' says Rhiannon. 'He'd buy some wine from Tesco, and say, "Right, we're having a wine-tasting." He'd stand there and say, "This is a lovely fruity red," making stuff up about the top notes and flavours and we had to guess the price before saying if we liked it. It was hysterical.'

One of Mo's most legendary nights was flower-arranging. He booked a local florist to come and talk to the girls for a couple of hours and show them how to do one arrangement but when, for the third week in row, and at short notice, she cancelled, Mo had had enough. 'He taught himself how to do the arrangement in just two days,' says Mandy. 'He tried to convince all of us that he had worked as a florist, but we could see he had notes pinned on the side of the table. It was brilliant but, to be honest, it was Mo's humour that kept our spirits up as much as the evenings themselves. If Mo wants to do something, he does it himself and they were incredible nights. We also had a Friday coffee morning, and every other Wednesday, every other Saturday there was something going on. It was fantastic.'

There are also the more sedate and perhaps serious welfare nights – I was invited to one of these by Kirsty who, feeling shy and not knowing many of the other wives, asked me to come along for moral support. The comfortable sitting room of the welfare house was filled with wives, children and a cheerful roar of chatter that immediately put Kirsty at her ease. Chairs were lined up facing a screen at one end of the room and, as the children were ushered into the room next door to watch some cartoons, Mo explained the formula for the evening. The welfare team had arranged for video cameras to be sent out to Afghanistan with the boys and now, a good month into their deployment, some footage had finally been sent back to show the wives how the men were living out there and let some of the soldiers send back personal messages. Private messages had also been filmed, which Mo had burned on to individual CDs for the wife in question to take home and watch without an audience. 'There won't be anything for me – we won't even see Ben,' Kirsty whispered, 'he would hate being filmed.'

There was an excited hush as the first face came on to the screen, the Commanding Officer of B Company, Major Paul, who spoke confidently into the camera, explaining how the company was split up, what each individual platoon was doing and what, as a whole, they were hoping to achieve during their time in Afghanistan. Behind Kirsty and I sat Sarah, Paul's wife, who looked a little embarrassed but pleased to see her husband's face. The film then moved on to the various PBs (Patrol Bases), where each of the platoons are stationed, a guided tour was given showing the wives where the men slept, ate and went to the toilet – the sight of which drew a collective 'urgh' from the room. Some of the braver men (those not afraid to taking a ribbing from their mates for showing affection) sent love direct into the camera to wives and children back home. Those wives in the room turned pink with pleasure while kids (most of whom had snuck back into the room, cartoons abandoned) shouted 'Daddy' if their father's face or voice came into the room. It was moving and uplifting and, noticing a tear in my eye, Kirsty gave me a mocking shove and said, 'Your husband's not even out there.'

After the film, parcels of fish and chips, battered sausages and beans (all pre-ordered on arrival and paid for by welfare) started to arrive while some wives went upstairs to the relative quiet of Mo's office to make video messages to be sent back to their husbands. A reporter from British Forces Broadcasting Service was there, giving the wives a chance to record a voice message which would be played on air on radio shows broadcasting out in Afghanistan. Children were noticeably more keen to do this, clamouring to tell daddy they loved him while the wives tended to hold back shyly.

Food was finished, tea drunk and the wives sat in companionable groups, tired smaller children draped over them, while the older ones still raced around from TV room back to mum and back again. I asked Kirsty what it felt like to see where Ben was. 'It was good,' said Kirsty. 'It didn't surprise me in the slightest not to see any of Ben, in fact I imagine Ben would be ducking and diving wherever possible to avoid the camera. I knew that he was living in quite primitive surroundings, so it didn't shock me and actually, when I think back to when Ben was in Sandhurst, in the middle of winter out in the pouring rain, digging himself a hole to sleep in, it doesn't seem so bad then. In fact it seems almost cosy out there, so yes it was good to see.'

They say that behind every brilliant man is an exhausted woman and I believe this is never more in evidence than in the army. Every happily married man out on the front line is, in part, able to do his job because of the support of a loving wife back home – 'The force behind the forces', as Amanda puts it. But even when the men are back in the UK that support continues. Mo's wife Clare is the perfect example of this; she is by Mo's side for every welfare event, throwing herself wholeheartedly into the role of welfare officer's wife and helping him to support the women whose husbands are away.

Clare's story is an unusual one – she first joined the battalion not as an army wife, but as a soldier. An infantry battalion, 2 R Welsh does not have any female fighting soldiers but the roles within the battalion of clerks, mechanics, chefs and medics can be filled by women who have trained alongside the boys. Clare joined as a lance corporal in 2000 and although at first she felt that the battalion was not quite sure what to do with a female in the ranks, she soon settled in. Mo was a colour sergeant (one of the more senior-ranking soldiers) and it soon became evident that despite the rank difference, the two had feelings for one another. 'I was booking ferry tickets for Mo when one of the civilian clerks pointed out, "Every time that Colour Sergeant Mo walks in, you blush." I said, "Get away!"' remembers Clare fondly. 'But that was it, we were match-made by that civvy clerk and her soldier husband. We had to sneak around for a bit because our rank difference meant that Mo shouldn't really have gone out with me, but after a year or so Mo spoke to the commanding officer and he was fine about it.' The couple married in 2002 and four years later their first child, Ryan, was born. 'And that was it,' says Clare. 'I stopped armying and started armywifeing.'

Clare hasn't looked back – at the welfare night I attended with Kirsty and at a coffee morning a week later, she was at the heart of everything, holding her four-month-old daughter Kimberley in one arm while making teas, introducing people and making sure that every wife there was being included.

'As welfare officer's wife I took on the coffee mornings – it was not an issue. Sometimes wives will say something to me because they don't want to bother Mo – they don't think it involves him. It could be something that they're struggling with, perhaps to do with their children. They don't realise that there are a lot of agencies that Mo's just got to phone and they can be round to help. If anything, I can be a go-between, especially for the new young wives. Mo's probably very daunting, because if their husband's a private or a lance corporal, they'd think, "That's a captain." You've auto-matically got the rank structure because the husbands would say, "Don't bother – don't see an officer." So it's ideal that I can be go-between – and it helps that I've had the connection with the battalion. A lot of the guys knew me when I was a lance corporal and a corporal, so they say, "Go and speak to Clare." I'm not an officer's wife in their eyes – I'm just Clare the clerk. It's eight years since I left the battalion, but for a lot of them I'm still Clare the clerk'

It is a full-time job, but one that Clare loves. 'The fun bits are seeing the girls get together,' she says. 'You've got women walking in, clinging on to their children, because they're the only people they know, then, by the end of the day, you can see the groups forming – it's not cliquey, but they start to bond. Then at the next event, nobody is stood on their own. The A Company wives continue to go out in the evening as a group – they made a pact that when their guys came home they'd go out for a meal every month, and they still do it. It's lovely, and I hope that B Company does the same.'

Although wives are not expected to take on the roles of their husband or their ranks – in fact wives who act superior to others due to their other half's senior status within the regiment are quietly frowned upon – inevitably the job your husband has will shape the role you yourself play in the battalion. I remember my mother-in-law Sarah, a retired colonel's wife, telling me how when my father-in-law commanded his battalion it was a full-time job for her too – hosting dinner parties, entertaining, looking after her family but also ensuring that all aspects of the wives' club ran smoothly and that everyone – from a private's wife all the way up – was looked after.

For the wife of the regimental sergeant major (RSM), the

most senior soldier (not officer) in the battalion, it is also a full-time job. Two of the Daffodil Girls have played the role of RSM's wife and had very different experiences. Amanda's husband was RSM when the battalion deployed as a whole to Iraq in 2007. She describes it as being like a 'big sister' to the other wives and she became heavily involved in the welfare side of the regiment, taking on the running of the weekly coffee mornings. 'We had a really nice community feel; because all the men were deployed, a lot of wives went back to Wales to live, but the core wives stuck around. It made the tour bearable and we stuck together, did a lot together, had a good sense of unity.'

Amanda wasn't working so had the time and energy to throw herself into helping to organise welfare trips, bingo nights and weekly coffee mornings. She also made sure she visited as many wives as possible so they knew she was a person that they could come and speak with should they need to. They raised money as well – holding raffles and cake sales to help with the running of the wives' club but also to ensure that, were the worst to happen, there was money in the kitty for every eventuality. 'We knew that we were going to lose boys,' explains Amanda, 'and we wanted to make sure we could provide something, as a community, if anything happened, such as memorials, something for the kids if their father was injured or killed. You hoped that it was just a contingency – we hoped we'd never need to use it. But, unfortunately, we did.'

For Julie, the role of RSM's wife came at the same time as she got a promotion to supervisor at a cleaning firm, her 'real' job. 'I struggled badly,' she remembers. 'I'm one person, with a family, trying to look after them and trying to help other people – and I found it very hard. I was stretched too thin emotionally and time-wise.' She found herself worrying about everyone and feeling that she couldn't be there for everyone as much as she wanted to. Julie was also maybe more shy than friend Amanda. 'I'd have to chair the wives' clubs meetings and I found it hard,' she says. 'I've always been one to be in the background – I've never needed to be at the front, and when I was put there I struggled badly and couldn't deal with it.'

Mandy was company sergeant major's wife when A company deployed to Afghanistan. Although not quite as senior as RSM, as the battalion only had one company deployed, Mandy's husband was the highest-ranking soldier away – so the role of company 'big sister' naturally fell to her. 'I wanted to do so much for the other wives,' she explains. 'I wanted to support them. It kept me busy but I hope at the end of it all, my experience and what I tried to do to help some of the younger ones helped them through the six months. I like to think it did.'

Wives like Amanda, Clare and Mandy are well suited to playing the role of regimental 'big sister', using their status within the wives' community to help, without taking on their husband's rank. But Simone tells me it didn't always used to be that way. 'There used to be stigma attached [to lower ranks] in the wives' club. When I was a young wife, married to a private, in those days even a corporal was "God". That's the way it was back then – company sergeant majors' and officers' wives were the mainstay of the wives' club. That was the score for the first ten years of me being an army wife. Not that there was anything wrong with that, but I just wasn't comfortable.'

Mandy agrees but hopes it has changed, 'Sometimes there's a stigma – some of the younger wives think, "Oh, my God, I can't go and talk to sergeant major so-and-so's wife, or a commanding officer's wife. You don't mix with them." But it's not like that at all, and I tried my damnedest to prove that to them. I became friends with one lady whose husband was a private in the company. When she told her husband, he said to her, "My God, you can't be friends with her. She's a sergeant major's wife." She just said, "Shut up! I like her – she's nice." And we stayed friends.'

As far as Mandy is concerned, when the men are deployed all the wives are in the same boat and should help each other out. 'Women don't have their husbands' ranks, and that's what I work on,' she says. 'I just saw it as trying to guide and help them in any way I could to get through this next six months. We all had someone there that we loved and we were all living the same – I won't say "hell" – it wasn't that, because we tried to make it through the best we could, in the only way we know how. Another way I look at it, a lot of those young women whose husbands are the privates, corporals and lance corporals, are this British Army's future. In the next ten or twenty years, our husbands will most likely be gone and we'll be living somewhere by the sea. They're going to be the ones guiding the new wives in. If any of them can take away something I've given them during that six months, I've done what I can.'

Julie feels the same as Mandy. 'I don't want to take on my husband's rank; my husband's job is his job, and my job is mine. I don't understand why wives take on their husband's rank. I'm friends with people who are privates' wives – I'm not going to not bother with them because they're privates' wives – because they're my friends and it's not different now Dai's an officer.'

After the welfare and 'Big Sister' wives, the life-blood of the wives' club is, of course, the wives themselves. I have already written about how neighbours and friends on the patch will gear up, looking after one another when the men first go away, but the more time I spend on the patch the more I have realised that the support continues throughout the tour and even when the boys return home.

Kaz, lying exhausted on the sofa, barely had the energy to rise even to make a cup of tea. It had been two days and her multiple sclerosis was making her lethargic and exhausted. Stress made it worse and this was a very stressful time: she and her husband Brian had not been getting on well and had decided that, for the time being, they should not have any contact. Brian had been posted away for a year, leaving Kaz to have their quarter while they worked out what they were going to do. 'Things weren't very good at all,' explains Kaz sadly, 'so we stayed away from each other, even though we were still married. We took that decision – we wanted to see where it was going. It was a really sad time, and I was very ill then.'

With Megan away at school, Kaz was very alone in the place she had really began to feel was home. Leaning down to grab her laptop which she always kept handy, feeling it gave her a link to the outside world, she logged on to Facebook and typed 'Not feeling well today ' as a status update, then, within minutes, the telephone rang – it was Elaine calling to see if she needed anything. 'It is always like that,' says Kaz, 'one or more of the girls will phone me and see if there's anything I need. Elaine is marvellous, I can call on her any time I want, and Amanda – I can just pick up the phone and they come over.'

During this particular bout of illness, when she and Brian had split up, Kaz also developed pneumonia – she was completely housebound, relying on her friends on the patch for everything from doing the shopping to keeping her company. 'Elaine used to go every day from work to Tesco to bring me home food,' Kaz explains. 'She doesn't have a car, so it was really out of the way and quite a walk.'

In return, when Kaz is well and driving, she offers her help in any way she can, 'If someone needs to go to town they'll phone me up and I will happily give them a lift. Or if they've got a day off and want someone to look after the children, they send them up here. It's like a little family. You don't get this kind of community elsewhere – it's a different thing with the army wives.'

Rightfully, the Daffodil Girls are proud of themselves, of their community and, of course, of their husbands. Sian has only ever known life in this world – where neighbours help one another out and loved ones go away for many months at a time. I met with Sian at her mother Dereynn's house. Sian's husband had just gone away for three weeks' training so Sian had returned home to mum. 'Dad's in Afghanistan and Alex is away, so it makes sense for mum and I to keep one another company,' she explains. I asked her what made her want to marry a soldier after witnessing the separations her parents are still having to go through? The answer was a straightforward one, and easy to identify with. 'I feel very, very proud – that I've grown up in the army and I've witnessed my dad doing what he loves doing, knowing that any minute it could all be over, but he's done what he loved. I'm crazy proud that I married into it – I think, "I must be stupid or potty," but I love it. There's nothing else out there. You go shopping and see a man in uniform and you think, "I want to shake your hand for what you're doing." There's a pride that I know my dad and husband are doing it. They're heroes every day.'

Out in the real world it is unlikely that our paths would ever have crossed – on paper at least, Sian and I would have had nothing in common. But, sitting on a sofa in a terraced house in the Matthews estate, I realise I have more in common with this smiley twenty-four-year-old than so many of the media types I called friends when I lived in London. There is an immediate bond between us because we are both in the same club – the club of army wives. Over a cup of sweet tea we talk about our dread of our husbands going away; Sian's husband is due to go to Afghanistan next year. I tell her that Ed is likely to be away for at best two months next year – at worst six, with time, potentially, in Afghanistan. At this point mum Dereynn joins us, 'Don't worry, hun,' she says, 'you can call on us any time.' And I know she means it.

Despite the best intention of friends living in the real world, it is impossible to understand what it is like to wave goodbye to the person you love for months at a time. Well-meaning platitudes can make a wife feel worse and thoughtless comments provoke tears; friendships can wane and you find that the army wife neighbour, who just weeks ago was a mere acquaintance, now understands you better than an old pal.

Sian, having grown up in the army, sums it up perfectly. 'This is the only life I've ever known,' she says, 'and I get really angry when people in Civvy Street complain – "My husband has to go away at the weekend on business, and he doesn't come back until Monday night," and I think, "Try having a husband away for six months, in a dangerous country, getting shot at. Try that for a long weekend and come back and tell me you're not happy." You feel like slapping them sometimes. I want to say, "You have no right to complain. Come and join our world as army wives, and then realise how hard it is – not having your husband there for a weekend, or one, two, three, four, six months of the year – then tell me how hard it is for you." I think people on Civvy Street believe it is somehow easier for us because we chose to marry a soldier but you don't choose who you fall in love with and you certainly don't choose to be parted from them. As the daughter of a soldier I knew what it would be like, but that doesn't mean it is any easier for me when my husband is away. Luckily we are surrounded by other women who DO understand and that is why this is my life – and the people living in the houses out there, they're my friends, my family.'

CHAPTER 3

'Love You, Miss You.
Not A Lot Happening Here . . .'

When Ed was deployed in Iraq, part of my morning routine was scanning the doormat for a glimpse of blue, which would mean that there was an airmail letter – known as a bluey – from Ed waiting for me. In turn, I wrote to Ed every morning using the fantastic 'e-bluey' system, which allows the user to write a letter as you would an email before sending it to the address where your loved one is stationed. Then, out in the field, the letters are printed up in a base as close as possible to the recipient. Sealed like a pay slip would be – making them completely private – the letters get to their destination far quicker, avoiding going through Royal Mail in the UK and then being flown to Afghanistan, than a normal bluey would. When Ed was stationed in Basra, the main British camp in Iraq, he once received one of my letters within three hours and even when he was out in the desert, patrolling the Iraq/Iran boarder and miles from any e-bluey printer, post would be sent with the food and water drops; he would normally get my missive, within a week of me writing them. The letters get to Afghanistan immediately, thanks to the world wide web and they can be printed up and forwarded on to the camps without access to email. Ed tells me that having a physical letter to hold is so much nicer than reading an email on a computer and the fact you can also add photographs makes this system invaluable. E-blueys can also be sent back to the UK, but in my experience most men still send the traditional handwritten bluey, preferring to rely on pen and ink rather than a potentially unstable internet connection out in the desert.

The e-bluey is a fantastic technological advance and one which has made a huge difference to serving military personnel and their families. But of course it wasn't always like that – my mother-in-law used to tell me horror stories of going for weeks without hearing anything from her husband, of the days when the men would often go months without access to a phone and letters took weeks, not days, to be delivered.

The longest-serving Daffodil Girls have also lived through these changes. In the early Nineties, when Simone's husband deployed to South Georgia, in the South Atlantic, on operational tour, the couple didn't even get to speak to one another on the phone. Left at home with their young son, Simone had to wait around six weeks for letters to arrive in either direction – a complete contrast to the fast, efficient e-bluey system. The only other means of communication, Simone tells me, were 'fam-grams' which could only be fifteen words long. Simone explains, 'You'd go and collect them from the families' office and that was the only form of contact, so that was really hard. It was all so un-private as well – nothing like the e-blueys these days – whatever you wrote in that fam-gram, everybody would see it. You'd write, 'Hope you're OK. Love you, miss you. Not a lot happening here. Kids are OK,' cramming as much as you could into your fifteen-word allowance, but not really able to say much at all. We were allowed about three of these a week – forty-five words a week to communicate with your husband. It was really horrible and it was my first tour.'

My husband's family has so much folklore on the nightmares of communication between my father-in-law Robin and mother-in-law Sarah that at times I was convinced they were trying to put me off marrying their son. In the late Seventies, Robin was on tour to Cyprus and Sarah, discovering she was pregnant with their first child, had no option but to tell her husband by letter – waiting three weeks for his reply. Then, when Robin went to the Falklands in 1987 for sixteen weeks, the couple managed to conduct a row by letter, their only means of communication. Sarah wrote to Robin to tell him she wanted to invest some of their money in the shares of a company she heard were going to do really well. The letter took three weeks to reach Robin, who responded immediately that she was not to take anything out of their savings until his return. By the time his reply letter reached Sarah, six weeks had passed since she first wrote and the money was long withdrawn and invested – she wrote back to tell him this. Another six weeks passed before she received his furious reply but by this point she was able to write back, rather smugly, that it had been a sound investment and they had made a decent amount of money. We laugh about this story now, but the undercurrent to me is how hard it must have been for Sarah, with two children under ten years of age, running the family and making important decisions alone, the only contact from her husband being a letter that took three weeks to arrive.

In comparison, it almost feels as though modern-day army wives have it easy – of course this is not the case and despite access to satellite phones, out in the field, letters are still the communication method of choice. It is, in many ways, very romantic. I have bundles of handwritten letters from the times Ed has been away, as does he – you can almost chart the course of our relationship from the early days where, still playing it cool, a 'Looking forward to seeing you' was as soppy as either us would venture, to more recently when the page is punctuated with 'I love you', 'I miss you'. How many modern couples have that kind of record? Like Simone, Dereynn has been around long enough to still find the ease of the e-bluey system a novelty. 'I've got a drawer upstairs where I've got the first letters,' she explains, 'from his first tours, I've still got them – it's mad. It's easier to stay in touch now you've got computers and I find it quicker to write an e-bluey than a handwritten letter and it gets to them quicker too.'

Together with daughter Sian they try to make sure they send something to Taff almost daily – more so than ever this tour. 'Sian has been sending him pictures of the baby, his first grandchild, so he can see her. He is missing so much when she is this young, but e-blueys mean we can send him photographs regularly.'

Letters come both ways and it is touching to learn that the sight of a bluey never gets mundane. 'I'm waiting for letters from him now because he said he's sent some,' says Dereynn. 'When they land on the doorstep you feel, "Oh my God!" I tend to just leave it there and when I've got five quiet minutes, I'll sit down with a cup of tea and a fag and read it properly – really enjoy it. After twenty-odd years married, he still writes "I love you".'

Simone's husband Mark is also based in Camp Bastion, which means if Simone writes him an e-bluey in the evening he will receive it the next morning. 'The system is brilliant,' says Simone with a grin. 'All the news I'm telling him is still new when he gets it, and when "OP MINIMISE" is on [when communication is closed for operational reasons], even though he can't phone or get emails, he can still get e-blueys. I always try to send him a photo with his e-bluey – I just go through the computer and pick random ones. My oldest son also writes to him every night but my younger son, he's a bit harder to get to write – he's more interested in his Xbox. Knowing Mark is getting lots of post, and that he knows our news almost immediately makes me feel much closer to him. I write about ordinary things, just life at home – my day, what I've done, tell him about the kids, the dogs, the car, always how much I'm missing him and how much I love

Amanda and husband Lee at a mess do

Amanda and eldest daughter Megan

2 R Welsh welfare officer Mo and wife Clare

Dereynn with husband Taff

Sian at a wives' club activity

The next generation of Daffodil Girls: Dereynn's daughter Sian, with her husband Alex and their daughter Bailey-Mae

Craig with Bradley

Donna and Craig on their wedding day with son Bradley

Elaine and husband Pete

Julie with best friend
Dereynn

Julie with husband Dai

Kaz and husband Brian

Kirsty and Benedict on the day they got engaged

Kirsty, Benedict and baby Annabel, aged just three days old. The day after this picture was taken Benedict returned to Afghanistan

Kitty and Ed on their wedding day.
Image courtesy of Nick Holt

Above right: Kitty with friend and
Daffodil Girl Kirsty at the 2 R Welsh
Christmas party

Right: Kitty in Afghanistan. Image
courtesy of David O'Neill/ *Mail
on Sunday*

Mandy and husband Ian on a family
outing to Thorpe Park

Ian with the kids, Cerys and Shaun the
day he returned from Afghanistan

Rhiannon as Audrey Hepburn at a fancy dress party at Sandhurst

Above right: Rhiannon and Huw in Cuba post tour

Right: Rhiannon and Huw at a mess do

Sarah and son James at his passing out parade

James on tour in Afghanistan

Simone and Amanda at a Help for Heroes concert

Simone and husband Mark at a mess do

Simone and family. From left to right: Dale, husband Mark, Simone and Brad

The 2 R Welsh

The wives' club group includes Dereynn, second from left, Sian, third from right, and Julie on the right

A day of playing soldiers – the wives' exercise

him. Other days when I'm feeling really down, I say, "Please come home." I know it's a silly thing to say, because he can't, but sometimes it helps to write it.'

Benedict has been making a concerted effort to write to Kirsty once a week. 'He's not soppy,' says Kirsty with a smile, 'but he is sweet – mainly putting my mind to rest, reassuring me, telling me the things it isn't safe to say over the phone.' The couple, however, still find it frustrating because it is impossible to be up to date – even with the e-bluey system. Ben's camp is so remote that Kirsty's letters (she normally writes around five a week) take up to ten days to reach him and Ben's letters take on average two weeks to get home. More often than not, a phone call will come before a letter, meaning the news Kirsty has lovingly written is out of date by the time it reaches Ben. However, this doesn't stop the post being a highlight of Ben's week.

Knowing this, I decided to write to Ben, a jokey letter about the adventures of Kirsty and their dog Lucy and taking the chance to ask him, in his own words, what letters mean to him. This was his response, 'I can't describe how exciting it is when the post bag arrives, the Patrol Base we are in is quite remote so all the post is flown in by helicopter, meaning that sometimes I am two weeks behind on the news from back home. Hearing from Kirsty, my parents or any friends who write can make a rubbish day into a good one, it is good to know people at home are thinking about me and helps to keep morale high. We finally got mail yesterday after a couple of weeks – I think I had about ten letters and two parcels from Kirsty, your letter – in total we had twenty bags for the platoon. I went to collect it with some of my soldiers in the middle of the night and we sorted it all and put each soldier's pile next to his bed while he was sleeping. So in the morning it was like Christmas! I think yesterday was one of the happiest we've had in our platoon base.'

Many of those letters left at the foot of the bed were written not by girlfriends or wives, but mothers. Most of the men sent away have a mother back at home who is every bit as worried as the wives in Tidworth, and for those single boys (and so many of them are just boys) letters from mum (and friends) are the only support he will receive in the long six months away.

When Sarah's twenty-one-year-old son James went to Afghanistan she wrote to him as often as she could, sending e-blueys around three times per week and encouraging James's younger brother and older sister to do the same. She filled them with local gossip, news from his friends – a diary of life at home. Together with daughter Emma, she would lovingly put together a package to send him weekly, filled with his favourite Haribo sweets, and anything he could make with hot water to add variation to his army diet. 'One phone call he asked me if I would send him out some Febreze,' Sarah remembers with a smile. 'I said, "Why would you want me to send that?" and he explained that they had no hot water at the FOB (forward operating base) and they could only use the showers two or three times a week – and he said, "I stink, and my clothes stink. I try to wash them, but they still stink." So Emma and I sent some Febreze, all the way to Afghanistan.'

*

E-blueys aren't the only technological innovation that helps modern army couples keep in touch. Some soldiers aren't naturally great letter writers, but with the growth of the internet and social networking sites, there are now other ways husbands and wives can communicate with each other.

Kaz's Brian is rubbish at writing home – Kaz tries to write to him most days and, because she is medically retired due to her MS, it is easier for her than for some wives to find the time to sit down and send her husband the latest news. Last tour Brian only wrote back eleven times in six months and, says Kaz, 'Five of them all came in one week after I moaned at him that he hadn't sent me any letters. It's not because he doesn't care, he just isn't good at writing. He'd say it was almost impossible – he'd be on guard, then he'd have two hours' sleep, then they'd be back again doing what they had to do, so they had very little time to put pen to paper the last tour. Anyway I'd prefer him to ring – to hear his voice.'

On this latest tour Brian has been based in the main Bastion camp with easier access to the internet, and Facebook has become the couple's preferred method of communication. 'It's nice,' says Kaz, 'most days he leaves me a message there; as I've said, he's not one for letter writing, but he communicates with me more now through the internet than on any of the tours he's been on. On his "wall" I can read the banter between him and the gang he's with out there and they seem to be really upbeat. I joke to him that you'd swear he's on holiday in Benidorm, not in Afghanistan. The other day I put something on about sunbathing, and he said, "Sunbathing, you fool, it's that hot over here I could cook an egg," and I said, "At least you'll be able to cook an egg when you come home, then," because he's a hopeless cook. Feeling that in some small way we are checking in with one another daily, and he knows what I am up to, makes things a lot easier.'

For Rhiannon and Huw, meanwhile, their preferred means of communication is the Paradigm email system. All the forward operating bases have two satellite phones and linked to them is a system where, instead of using your phone minutes to make calls, you can send emails instead. Rhiannon explains to me how it works, 'There are two terminals as well as the phones, and they have to send you an email first – I couldn't just send him one. He could send me one and then I could reply – that's a security thing. The email can only be four megabytes and there's quite a learning curve when you start doing it. You'd be writing away and then that wouldn't send – then you take out all the punctuation, then lots of words to get it small enough that it would go. Then you'd get the hang of it after a while – how much you can write.' Rhiannon has also had to get used to what she can and can't say. 'Even on secure systems you have to be careful – no names, or places or dates. So if you're talking about when they are due to fly home they'd have to say, "It'll be the fourth day after your birthday." It's a bit tricky sometimes and I'd completely mess it up and write, "Oh, on the 6th."'

Computer problems, though, do not just happen on Civvy Street. 'There was a period when Huw's account broke,' she recalls. 'They'd got a new machine, and if you wanted to use the new one you had to re-set-up on it. No one wanted to do it, and so Huw threw himself on the wire and did it and somehow his account got corrupted. He could send me messages, but he wasn't getting mine back. I was getting more and more frantic ones from him. "I don't know if you're getting these." And I was writing back, "They're coming through, we just can't get back to you." I think it might have been over two weeks and that was quite difficult, both because although I was getting the messages from him they had no information in, just "Are you getting these?" and because of not being able to send anything back. That was frustrating.'

These technological hitches aside, Rhiannon is full of praise for the system, 'It's good to see messages in my inbox – I'd also get them at work as he cc'd them to my work address and so I'd get two replies that I could make. I'd have spares then. He'd also send me blank ones to reply to so then I could email when I wanted to. I'd write – nothing very romantic, as we're not that way inclined – but it was good to be able to check in with one another so easily.'

Parcels are another way for family to show their love and support for a soldier – and of course receiving one is a welcome break to the monotony of army camp life. When Ed was in Iraq I would send a parcel weekly, adhering to the strict rule that it had to be under 2 kg, I would rack my brain with what to fill it with, sending, I hoped, clever and entertaining things to make him smile, if even for a moment. At this point, in 2007, you still had to pay for parcels (around £7 for 2 kg – a lot for a wife on a low or no wage) until a campaign by an army mother persuaded Royal Mail to drop all postage costs for post sent to members of our armed forces serving in Afghanistan or Iraq, making it far easier for family, friends and a battalion's welfare team to send out parcels of goodies.

As well as looking after the wives left behind, Mo, Clare and the welfare team work hard to give the men in Afghanistan a much-needed morale boost; as well as arranging for video messages to be sent out, Clare organises a production line of wives to pack and send parcels – ensuring that even those young men without wives or close family know that they are being thought of back home.

'We have sorters and weighers,' Clare explains. 'No parcel can be over 2 kg and we were told by the ladies at the post office that if we make them 1.5 kg they can fit more in a postal sack, meaning they get delivered quicker. We send all kinds of things: shower gel, sweets, magazines, anything like that really – from A Company we had two mums who bombarded every company and supermarket local to them in Wales and got lots of goodies donated. Mo went down and collected it all and the local paper took photos – in total they collected enough to make 501 shoeboxes. We also had the help of three schoolteachers in Wales who got their children to make boxes – those were lovely, filled with things such as conkers and drawings. The children would cover the shoeboxes with stickers and drawings —the little girls would put little love hearts. These boxes took us a long time to sort and wrap because we were all stopping to say "Ahhhhh – look at this," and Mo would come down and say, "All I can hear is 'ahhhh'. Stop 'ahhhhhing' and get wrapping." The best boxes to wrap are the children's.'

For the men out in the field it is not so much the stuff in the parcel as the fact that people back home have taken the time to send them. 'I don't think the guys knew how much support they had,' says Clare, 'then they received all these parcels – so many goodies, to the point that they were literally giving stuff away to other regiments and battalions because they had too much. It was absolutely brilliant and they were very touched.'

Before being taken to the post office the boxes had to be packed or those that had been donated had to be sorted through to check nothing unsuitable was being sent (such as aerosols which might explode on the flight) before being wrapped in brown paper. Clare was pregnant with Kimberley at this point and in the morning, while son Ryan was at pre-school, she would grab the chance to get some serious wrapping done. In the afternoon other wives would join her with their children. 'Ryan and I found we could wrap five parcels together in an hour,' she remembers with a grin. 'Ryan likes to hold the paper, and just before you put the tape on, he goes, "Surprise!" Other wives with small children were doing this as well, so it was all quite fun and in a strange way relaxing. The only downside was that people had Christmas presents to wrap but they couldn't face it when they got home, because they were fed up with wrapping.'

Initially the parcel drive by 2 R Welsh was for Christmas. The welfare team and wives sold rubber wristbands with 'Support the R Welsh in Afghanistan' to collect money to send out some extras for the guys to have with their Christmas dinner. 'Just crackers and decorations, so they could put a bit of tinsel up, and we made sure every soldier had a Christmas hat,' says Clare. 'But the response was so phenomenal we could have sent the parcels at any time of year.'

Most wives, and mothers for that matter, would agree there are very few 'highs' when the son or husband you love is out in a war zone. If there are, they come in the form of letters home or the longed-for phone call. But even this is fraught with difficulties. Imagine the worst mobile reception you have ever had, and then double it – a call from Afghanistan really is like a call from another world, particularly for those out in the field relying on a satellite phone. I remember Ed calling me once from the desert in Iraq during a sandstorm, sheltering by the side of his WIMIK, the stripped down Land Rover which was his transport and home for weeks at a time. He had leapt at the chance to use the phone and I could barely hear through the howling gale and terrible static – it was good to hear his voice, know he was OK, but so frustrating not being able to communicate properly, especially when I knew this might be my only phone call that fortnight.

Far worse than getting a call when you can hardly hear your loved one, or not getting a call at all, is when you miss one – it is, quite simply, terrible. You know that, miles from home, your beloved has tried to get hold of you and you feel that, by not being there, you have failed them. The guys get thirty free minutes a week to call home (which you can pay to top up) but actually being able to use these minutes can often be a challenge; soldiers sometimes having to queue for ages in camp, or waiting for days out in the field to get their turn and it is unbearable to think of them only getting through to an answer machine.

I would throw what can only be described as a tantrum when I missed a call – it is always a UK-seeming number that flashes up on your mobile but call it back and a recorded voice informs you that 'Someone serving in the armed forces has tried to call you . . .' To try and avoid ever hearing that message your phone goes everywhere with you, and I mean everywhere – to the loo, left on loud in meetings, placed on the bar when out with friends. I remember once leaving it on my desk while I went downstairs for a coffee while working at the *Mail on Sunday* – returning to the missed call, I burst into tears and my editor (an amazing woman who managed to be a fantastic section editor and a wonderful boss – unusual, believe me) pulled me into her office and let me sob on her shoulder.

Rhiannon's bosses also completely understood and, despite Rhiannon being relatively new, didn't mind that her phone would always be switched on and prominently placed on her desk, to try and ensure she wouldn't miss a call from Huw. When one came, she would run from her desk to stand on the landing outside the main office of the accountancy firm where she works, covering her free ear with one hand to try to make the echoing satellite phone link bridge the distance between Salisbury and Helmand as much as possible. Neither Huw nor Rhiannon is one for soppiness on the phone – it was more a chance to catch up, however briefly, for Huw to reassure his wife that he was OK and for her to do likewise. Of course they always said 'I love you' before hanging up. Yet despite the seemingly ordinary content, these precious phone calls were very private to Rhiannon. 'It had been a couple of weeks of me talking to Huw at the top of the landing by the open-plan staircase,' says Rhiannon 'I didn't realise that our receptionist and phone staff downstairs could all hear me talking. They said to me afterwards, "You know we can hear you?" They thought it was really sweet – but I had to go and find another spot to talk.'

Sarah missed the first phone call from son James – she was in a meeting so had her phone on silent. James left her a message, knowing how worried she had been, just reassuring her, 'Don't worry, everything's fine. We're all settled.' That night he called back, he was in Bastion and went to great pains to let his mum know that he was OK. 'He'd even had a pizza for his tea,' says Sarah. 'I was amazed that there was a Pizza Hut in Camp Bastion. He said it was unbelievably hot, but that him and his mates were OK.' Like most young men, James wasn't great at chatting on the phone and Sarah knew she wouldn't get a letter from him but she was happy just to hear his voice, however briefly.

All loved ones feel the same – the content of the phone call is not as important as actually hearing the person's voice. Even after so many tours a phone call still lifts Dereynn's day. 'The first thing we say is, "How are you doing?" There's usually been a lot going on, but Taff doesn't explain just says it's busy, then he asks what I've been up to. He'll always ask how the baby, his granddaughter, is doing. So I joke, "So you don't want to know about your wife, then?" He does of course – but he asks how the baby's doing. It makes me laugh, at the end of the conversation he says he's going to go, and he asks one last time, "How's Charlie?" Charlie's the dog. "How's Jasper?" That's the cat. Then, "How's Bailey? Give her a kiss from me" – that's the baby. Then he asks about Sian and Gavin, our two kids, then me – I'm just the wife.' Dereynn knows that asking about the cat and dog makes Taff feel closer to the family he has had to leave behind. 'At the end he always says, "Love you," and I say, "Love you . . . bye." He is a soppy old sod really. When you put the phone down you think, "That was quick" and then you're just waiting for the next time that he phones.'

Donna tried not to think about the fact that husband Craig was in a war zone. She put it to the back of her mind and carried on with her day-to-day life looking after son Bradley and (almost pretending that Craig was just training somewhere in the UK). But when he called, of course, the static line was an all-too-clear reminder of how far apart they were. The couple talked about how much they missed one another, home-coming plans and what they were going to do for their first wedding anniversary. 'He didn't talk a lot about himself,' says Donna, 'he just wanted to know what was going on our end and how his family was.' Occasionally Craig would ring in time to speak to three-year-old Bradley before he went to bed but more often than not he would call in the evening and the newlyweds would enjoy about twenty minutes of conversation before he had to hang up. 'Sometimes he'd phone me at five o'clock in the morning, just to tell me he was back in from patrol,' recalls Donna, 'which was lovely, but I'd think, "I was sleeping – I wasn't worrying." And I did worry, despite trying not to think about it, because I had a sort of gut feeling – but that was because I knew the risks.'

If your husband is out on the front line it is hard, when you put down the phone, not to worry that that could be the last time you speak to them. Julie tells me that she advises all wives that, no matter what, their last words on the phone to their husband should always be "I love you"; 'Even if you're angry with him,' she says. 'Because sometimes you're on the phone and you ARE angry with them. They're over there and we're over here, looking after the children and you can get cross with them for leaving you even though you know it is not their choice. But no matter what, I knew that if anything did happen to Dai, the last thing I would have said to him was "I love you" and no matter how tense our conversation had been I would know that he knew.'

CHAPTER 4

'My God – Our Dad's Out There'

Megan doesn't remember the first time her father went away; she was far too young, but in the videos that chronicle their family history is a clear record. It is Lee that drives the home videos – Amanda rarely bothers to get the camera out when he is away – so the gaps in the films tell their own story of his absence. The earliest video of Megan shows a beaming, chubby baby just crawling and starting to try to exchange words with Lee, off-screen as he was manning the camera, the pride clearly audible in his voice. In the next video Megan is walking and a man who is now a stranger confuses the toddler as he asks her to wave for the camera. 'It must have been six months later and he'd been to Canada,' recalls Megan, 'I was walking and I didn't know who he was. That really upset him: I just wanted my mum, I didn't want to look at him and I was hiding away because I didn't know who he was.'

It is not only wives that the soldiers of 2 Royal Welsh leave behind when they are deployed abroad. For many, there are families to say goodbye to as well. Living in Tidworth, it is always noticeable how many children there are in the town; babes in arms, toddlers sitting upright in their mum's shopping trolley while she does the weekly shop in Tesco, children playing in the street and teenagers trying to look cool, hanging out in groups outside the fish and chip shop. In Tidworth there are countless boys and girls who are having to be brave, but in a different way to their fathers, growing up faster than children on Civvy Street, aware from a young age that the world can be a scary and dangerous place, where dads go away for months on end and some don't come home.

The life of an army child is something I struggle to imagine – I was educated in a local school and despite both my parents having very full careers was never separated from one or other for more than a month. A self-confessed daddy's girl, I remember being stricken when my father was away for work for long periods of time and even now, in my thirties, I am still very close to both my parents, speaking to my mother almost daily. Mum or dad were there for every (hated) sports day, parents' evening or school play. After school, mum and I would sit at the kitchen table and over a cup of tea and slice of toast I would tell her about my day, I remember both helping me with my homework (Mum – English and art, Dad – maths and history). Dad and I would have tearful (me, not him) rows when he stood over me making me do my piano practice and mum invented 'book and art' clubs encouraging my brother and I to read and be creative in our spare time. It was dad who dropped me off at my first teenage disco and, when he came to collect me, discovered me kissing a boy so gave me the 'birds and bees' chat awkwardly when he got me home. It was on both their shoulders I cried over my first broken heart.

Mum and dad have been there every step of the way throughout my life. I rely on them hugely and, now I am older, them on me. In contrast, my husband Ed, a former army child, is very independent – he was sent to boarding school from the age of eight, to give his education some stability while the army moved the family around the world and is far less sentimental than I am about time spent with family or old mates. He tells me stories of half-term holidays spent at friends' houses (his parents were stationed in Canada and the budget couldn't stretch to mid-term flights), or rugby matches where he would play his best with no one at the side of the pitch cheering him on. No after-school chat with mum or dad for boarding school pupils, instead weekly letters and phone calls. Ed is close to his parents, but is more self-reliant than I can ever imagine being.

Ed's family was stationed in many places when he was growing up: various corners of the UK, Germany and as far afield as Canada. Sarah, Ed's mum always tells me proudly how they moved twenty-one times in her time as an army wife. It is an existence they have thrived on, but not one that I feel is for me. I love going back to my home town, returning to familiar haunts, meeting friends I have known since childhood – knowing that this is where I belong. For an army child – or patch brat, as many proudly nickname themselves – growing up is about countless moves, a boarding school education for many and, as they get older and more aware of the world, the anxiety that goes with having a parent in a war zone.

Megan's father, Lee, has been in the army since he was seventeen – the same age she is now. He has been away nine times in her short life yet despite this, or perhaps because of it, Megan and younger sister Bethan are very close to their father. When Lee is away the family tends to stop; according to Megan they just survive. 'Work, food, go out, sleep – until he comes back,' she explains. 'We want to try to climb Ben Nevis before he comes back, so we can say we've done something, but we don't want to do stuff when he's not here, because we do stuff as a family. If he's not here, it's not complete – in a way, our life's on hold.'

Sian is another Daffodil daughter who, like Megan, has grown up used to her father being away for months at a time. Of course when they were both children they may have missed their father but both girls say they were sheltered from the realities of what their father did for a living. 'When you're younger you don't realise the extent of what's happening,' says Sian. 'You're at an age where you're not fully aware of what's going on in the world, and as you grow up and you know where he's going, there's that realisation that it's a pretty big thing.'

It wasn't until Megan was fourteen, in 2007, and Lee went to Iraq that it really hit her where her dad was and what he was doing. 'Before that I don't remember him being away being so bad,' Megan says. 'The media brought it home to me and my sister – before, we didn't know how dangerous it was. But when he went to Iraq we were old enough – we'd watch the news and see the explosions, and we'd think, "My God – our dad's out there." It was really hard.'

For Sian, it was also a tour of Iraq – and the media coverage – that made her realise how dangerous her father's job was. He first went nine years ago when the family was based in Germany and Sian started to watch the news – constantly. 'That was a tough one for me – I'd not had any tough times before that, because I always had mum to fall back on. Even though I missed dad, she'd always say, "It's all right because he'll be back in a couple of months." The pivotal moment was when I was fourteen and it was on the news all the time – Iraq and what was going on. You'd read about deaths and I'd think, "My dad's not as invincible as I think he is. It could be him."'

As well as coping with separation and the angst of knowing their father is in a war zone, both Megan and Sian have had to cope with countless changes of home, school and friends when postings and relocation of the regiment meant their fathers' job forced a move. Megan has now been living in Tidworth for more than five years, spending all of her secondary school education at just one school, only ten minutes' outside Tidworth. But before that she had attended ten schools. 'It was OK when I was younger, I was quite bubbly and chatty so found it easy to make new friends but it was hard saying goodbye so often,' Megan recalls. 'Now though I think I will be able to stay and finish A-levels in one place, and even if we do get a posting, which I don't think will happen, we can ask not to move because I'm in the middle of A-levels. I do think all the moves affected my school work; not basic English and maths but things like German and art – when you had to leave all your work behind and start afresh and you're doing different topics that you haven't got a clue about. Then at the new school they're in the middle of the topics and you've got to go home and read through the whole thing on your own, so that was hard. But luckily I've been in the same secondary school the whole way through.'

Sian, whose father joined the army when she was three years old, started her life as a Daffodil daughter in Hong Kong. 'I remember being ripped away from all I'd ever known and I blamed my parents massively for that. I didn't adjust well at first and I hated my dad for a while – I thought it was so unfair, being posted every two years to different places. You're just settling in and making real friends, then they say there's a posting coming up. I moved school every time so I probably went to about seven different ones. I'd have to start again and make new friends and a new life – knowing you're not going to be there for long, you don't settle. You're more aware as you get older so you don't invest too much time in people – there's no point. You'll be moving again and there'll be more friends you'll lose contact with. My long-term friends are in the battalion – we all grew up together.'

Megan is very close to her mum, Amanda. I am touched to see this teenager posting on Facebook how much she loves her mum, how proud she is of her and the work she does at Help for Heroes. 'She's inspirational,' Megan states simply. 'I've always known she's caring and she helps everyone. Every one of her brothers and sisters has had help from her – she's the rock of the family.' For someone so young Megan is far more stoical than I have ever managed to be about army life; perhaps if this is the only world you have known it is easier to accept. Wiser than her years, Megan passes on some good advice to me, a relative newbie: 'It's happening and there's nothing we can do as individuals to stop it. It's going to happen – you've got to realise that you've got to be there for them while they try to be there for you as well. They're away, doing a hard thing but being home and waiting for six months is, I'd say, the harder thing.'

There are good points, though. Megan sees how the separations have made her mum and dad stronger as a couple. 'My parents are still quite loved up and sloppy,' she tells me. 'They're the kind of couple that like a night in together – they both have their hobbies, my mum likes bingo and my dad likes darts, so they do that on the same day each week so they don't have more than one night apart. Every other night it's a cup of tea and chocolate and a DVD and they cuddle up. They are so cute, I'd do anything for that sort of relationship with someone else when I'm older. I think the separations have made them stronger. When my dad's been away, my mum's trying to cope, but she can't because she misses him. But when he's back, she's fallen in love again and it's perfect. It goes back to normal, if not better.'

When I spoke to Megan, her dad Lee had been in Afghanistan for under a month and this tour was proving to be the hardest yet experience for this Daffodil daughter. The morning Lee left, Megan got up after his departure determined to face the day and crack on. She knows her dad loves what he does and that he is good at it, which brings some comfort, and instead of focusing on six long months she tried to think of it as three months without her dad, knowing that halfway through the tour he will be home for a two-week rest and recuperation (R&R) break. Three months doesn't feel so bad, and she hopes with college to keep her busy and Christmas to look forward to it will fly by. But downstairs Megan could hear Amanda crying, and she knew that at this point there were no words of comfort she could give her mum. 'I know that if it was my husband or boyfriend, it would be devastating.' Megan says, 'I know there's nothing I can do that's going to calm her down for the first four weeks. She says that's the worst. I try to be with her, be there for her as much as I can, and also stay out of the way, so that she can have a bit of her own time as well.'

Like her mother, Megan lives for her father's phone calls. Megan tends to pretend that her dad is just away training somewhere, blocking out that fact that he is in a war zone but even this doesn't stop his absence hitting home when he does eventually call. 'I'm stronger than I would have expected,' Megan explains, 'but when I'm talking on the phone there's a big lump in my throat and my voice starts shaking and I'm really sad. Then I put the phone down, have a quick cry and get it out, and get on until he calls next – and that's every two weeks. I don't mind crying once every two weeks.'

For both Megan and Sian, part of being a Daffodil daughter is looking out for their mother while their father is away.

The hardest thing about this tour, Megan says, is seeing how much her mum is suffering. 'I don't think our mum is taking it well,' Megan explains. 'I've seen her trying to be brave on the phone then getting off and crying her eyes out – that's probably the hardest part and there's nothing we can do that can change it. He can't come back even if we want him to and there's a big bit of life missing when he's away.'

Sian doesn't cry anymore; she used to sob on her father's return – the pent-up emotion of the previous months would prove too much and the relief she felt at his safe return would manifest itself in tears that had been held back the whole time he was away. 'Now,' she says, 'I haven't cried for a while, I think I block it out – I know he's going. Then he goes – and then you just get on with it and wait until he's back. I try to support my mum in the best way I can. This is the hardest tour for me, because of being away from home – this is the first tour my mum's done alone, without me being in the house. The thought of her being on her own panics me a bit but I talk to her every single day and we see each other all the time.'

Both Daffodil daughters are aware that it is not just during the tour that they need to be concerned about their parents, but afterwards too. 'When I was little and dad was away I missed him and it was a massive strain on everyone – mum having to be mum and dad at the same time, putting up with us and having the backlash,' explains Sian, 'and dad reaping all the benefits from it, the cuddles and kisses when he got back. I can sympathise with mum now and when Bailey gets bigger, she could say, "I hate you – I want my dad" and that will be me – how I was with my mum. I can imagine me having to be the bad guy, then my husband Alex getting all the benefits, getting all the cuddles and kisses because he is a novelty to her. It's like a tape going round in my head – it's payback time from me being an absolute nightmare to my mum.'

Megan knows, too, that after the relief of a homecoming there is a period of readjustment which is just as strange for the family as it is for the soldier. 'When my dad came back from Iraq for good it was a relief – he's back safe, it's so much easier to sleep, but then the routine starts going back to HIS routine, which can be hard sometimes for us to adjust to, because while he's away we get into our own routine without him.' Sian agrees, 'Dad is different when he comes back from tours – a few times he's come back and it's hard to adjust back to life at home. He's been away and mum's had to carry on – we've all got into a routine, and he comes back and there were times he tried to disrupt that routine and he's been put in his place by my mum. She tells him, "You've got to work into our routine." That's got to be hard on him as well as us, when he'd being doing God knows what in a world far different from the one we're used to.'

Megan's boyfriend is not in the army. Her father is notoriously protective and Megan tells me with a laugh that boys are not even allowed in the house. Lee always wanted his girls to end up with a policeman or soldier – someone he felt could protect them and Megan, always agreed – until now. 'I've always thought I'd marry a soldier,' she says, 'but after this tour, I don't think I would. I've seen my mum and the way she's been, how hard it really is, I understand now.'

All of the Daffodil mothers I have spoken to find their children to be a massive comfort when their husbands are away. When the children are younger, putting them first, being strong for them, forces their mother to cope better with the separations than perhaps they would if they were on their own. Elaine keeps things as normal as possible, to make dad's absence as painless as possible for their two young ones. Julie's children are older now but last time their dad Dai, went away they helped Julie cope with the tour. 'Friends get you through – they help you so much it's unbelievable,' she says, 'and the kids get you through it. You know you can't fall apart, because if you do and you've got little children, they can sense – and you don't want them feeling the same way you do. The kids make you strong.'

Simone's eldest son Dale is now nineteen and having him at home makes the months Mark is away more bearable. 'Now they support me,' she explains. 'I've always been very nervous of staying on my own at night – it sounds a bit melodramatic, but when I was younger, I would sleep with a knife under my pillow. I'm scared of someone breaking in – I'd lie awake for hours and hours at night. Since we've lived here, this is the safest I've ever felt – it may be partly that Dale's a young man now, and I've got his company, I don't feel alone at night anymore.'

After years of putting her children first it is now this Daffodil Girl's turn to be looked after by them and she has not been disappointed. When Simone came to my house for supper one evening, both her sons showed up on my doorstep to collect her when the meal was over – making sure she was accompanied even for the short walk back to their house and like a pair of bodyguards dwarfing their petite mum as they escorted her home.

*

I believe that a tour is harder for those wives who have younger children. For them, alongside the strain of their husband going away is the pressure of being, effectively, a single mum for up to six months of a year. Sian, who has watched her mum go through it for as long as she can remember, puts it like this, 'If you're an army wife it's definitely more of a role than a civvy wife. You're a wife, and a father, and electrician, chef, plumber – you have to do it all and support them while they're out there.' It is a sentiment shared with Julie, an older generation of Daffodil Girl, 'When they're away you're looking after two children and trying to be a mum, a dad, and even trying to be their grandparents too,' she tells me. 'You've got to be all that in one, and it's very, very hard.'

Elaine knows her husband loves his job and she supports him one hundred per cent despite the hardship it creates for her. 'I wouldn't stop him,' she says. 'I've spent two years effectively being a single mum, but you get used to it, you have to deal with it, being in the army. You can't have it any other way, as there will always be tours, and there'll be plenty more. I never feel times when I would like to be looked after because I'm the mum and wife – and that's what mums and wives do – they look after the husbands and the kids.'

Dereynn too echoes this response, 'Even now there are times when I could say, "I've had enough now, it's time for you to come home." But you still pick yourself up. You get used to being a single parent – you deal with things day to day, just you and the kids.' But, she tells me, as the children get older she has started to miss them being dependent on her, distracting her from her husband's absence. 'Now the kids are older I do feel less needed, you haven't got to think about them doing their homework, or being nursemaid when they are ill,' she says. 'They're independent in their own way – and it's harder, because I feel redundant, knowing I'll go to work, come home, and if Gav's not in I don't have to rally round getting packed lunches . . . getting tea sorted. It can be lonely. Sian lives with her husband now so it's only me and my son – I'm not relied on by anybody at the moment. I come home and there's nothing.'

For many of the men who go off to war the woman waiting at home for them is not a wife, but their mother. If I can imagine one thing worse than waving goodbye to your husband it would be saying goodbye to your son, knowing your child is going somewhere where you can't protect him. Ed's mum Sarah had said goodbye to her husband for years before she had to watch her son leave for Iraq. 'Just think "he has just gone to work" and not where that work is,' she advised me before his second tour, employing the coping mechanism that she had perfected over years of goodbyes. She tells me now that it was the goodbye she always hated, with both father and son, but once she had had that final hug and watched first her husband, then her son, walk away she would keep herself busy, forcing herself not to think about where they were. With Ed, she said, it was definitely harder. Although she had great faith in Ed's ability as a soldier, and in the army – and God – not to put him unnecessarily in harm's way, my husband, an impressive officer, was still her little boy. She also knew that as a younger officer he was more likely to be in more dangerous situations than his father, a colonel, had been during his last couple of tours.

On both occasions that Ed left for Iraq Sarah cried at his departure, but after that, that was it – she wouldn't allow herself to cry. She thought about her son every day but knew after years as an army wife that her worrying wouldn't make any difference so she kept busy rather than 'sat around in tears' as she puts it. Sarah may have listened to the news with a bit more attention than normal but when she would hear a bulletin saying that someone had been killed, after the initial heart stop, she was able to think logically that if it was something to do with Ed she would have heard by now. This ability to be calm, to keep busy and force yourself not to worry unnecessarily is something that can only be learned through practice but after thirty-four years of being married to a soldier, Sarah had had plenty of that.

Another Sarah, our Daffodil mother, had not had the same experience of the army world as my mother-in-law and was not able to deal with her son going away in the same way: she was devastated when she dropped her son James off at the gates to camp. On the way up from the family house in Wales he had told her he was nervous about going and sad to be leaving his friends and family for so many months. She couldn't bear seeing him so apprehensive and sad. Sarah hugged him goodbye fiercely, not wanting to let him go, then watched, stricken, as he rounded the corner on his own without turning back to look at his mum one last time. At twenty-one, James was a man in the eyes of the world but to Sarah he was still her baby. 'I told him I loved him, and he said he loved me – and that he'd be all right, then he was gone,' she says. 'I just sat there in the car, in pieces, to the point of thinking I had to go in and check he was OK – but I knew I wouldn't be able to get in. It was physically painful leaving him and watching him walk round the corner. I was handing him over to the unknown – to the enemy. No mother would put her child at risk and yet here I was, having to let him go.'

Sian, despite watching her parents go through the trial and tribulations of army life, married her own soldier in 2010 before giving birth to a daughter, Bailey-Mae, a few months later. Army daughter, wife and now mother Sian has, and will, experience every different emotion we women who are left behind can go through. Now, even though she has left home, she finds it harder to say goodbye to her dad Taff than when she was little – knowing that now it is not just her he is leaving, but also her baby girl, and realising that he will inevitably miss key moments in his beloved granddaughter's early life.

Sian always knew she would end up marrying someone in the military, even though her mother wasn't keen. 'When I was growing up, my mum always said, "Try not to marry a soldier, whatever you do. Try to find a nice lad who's not in the army." I didn't understand at the time why she said that, but now I'm married into it and a mum myself, I understand – she's been through it and still is – and now she has to witness her daughter going through what she did. It's her life passed down as she looks at me.'

Dereynn confirms this. 'It is hard. I watched her last year going through her first tour when Alex went to Afghanistan for six months. I was the brick for her – she's now married and got the little one, and even though she's in her own little place, she's being the little brick for me while my husband is away. When she fell in love with a soldier, part of me wanted to say to her, "Please don't get with a soldier. You've seen what your dad goes through. You've seen what happens . . ." It's like history repeating itself. Taff missed out on so much of her childhood and now he is missing out on Bailey-Mae's; by the time he gets back she's going to be that little bit older and bigger, we'll send him pictures but it is not the same. Then next year it will be Alex, Sian's husband, going away and he'll be missing out like Taff did – first with his daughter and now his granddaughter.'

Sian has been through countless tours as an army daughter but tells me that as a wife it is a completely different experience. 'It was absolute torment – it's a different relationship and even though they're both doing the same job, you have a completely different emotion for both of them. There's your dad going out there, and then it's your husband and you have this torment every day, day in, day out. When it was my dad, I could shut it down but when it's someone you're in love with, it's completely different – you think, "What's he doing? Is he OK? Where is he?" every minute of every day.'

Now she is a mum Sian is dreading Alex's next tour, to Afghanistan, especially as he is going to miss their little girl's first birthday and, Sian knows, undoubtedly many other important milestones in their daughter's life. 'When Bailey was born I looked at her and thought, "I want you to know your dad,"' Sian recalls. 'I don't want her to look at him after six months of not seeing him and wonder, "Who are you?" That freaks me out – the thought of him going away, and her not knowing who he is when he comes back – and him being utterly devastated because of that. It's going to be like being a single mum.'

Sian finally understands what her mother went though for all those years. 'I can see what my mum told me all along, about being a mother and a wife,' Sian says. 'She'd say to me, "When you have your kids, you'll understand what I went through," and now I have to say, "You know, mum – you were right in that," and I hate to say it. We don't like to admit our mums are right, but they are.'

CHAPTER 5

'You Enjoy R&R, But You Can't Relax . . . You Know They're Going Back'

It was before dawn when Rhiannon dragged herself out of bed and, despite her excitement, she felt exhausted. Pulling on a pair of jeans and a T-shirt she headed down to the car for the hour and a half drive to RAF Brize Norton where her husband Huw, home for two weeks from Afghanistan, was due to land at 6 am. She had never been to Brize before so it was with some frustration that she queued at the security gate to get a photo taken for a car pass – it was far too early for that kind of faffing. She drove through the barbed-wire-topped gates and, following the instructions she had been given, parked in front of the single-storey building that housed both the departure and arrivals lounges of the military airport.

Pushing through the revolving glass door to the left of the building Rhiannon found herself in the arrivals section of the terminal. It was five-thirty in the morning and the small cafe was closed, its shutters firmly down. The car hire desks were also shut and the collection of tables and chairs empty save for a couple of other hardy wives. A small barrier separated the seating area from the sliding doors, which would soon open to reveal the returning soldiers, but Rhiannon chose a table further back, nearer the entrance to the building. Attached to the wall a TV played out silent images from a news channels adding to the slightly desolate, deserted feel that the terminal had at this early hour.

Rhiannon had packed a flask of tea and was glad of it as she sat with her book and tried to focus on reading rather than Huw's imminent arrival But as other wives and families started to appear, Rhiannon all but gave up on her book, instead watching the women and children. It was announced that the flight had been delayed by twenty minutes and the excitement and tension in the room became tangible. Finally, they were told the plane had landed.

Slowly the men began to trickle though the double automatic doors which separated the arrivals from the baggage collection point, where the men had to wait for their bags like in a civilian airport – Rhiannon felt as though she had waited hours for Huw to come through. There were about three families there with children under seven and Rhiannon had been watching them, their growing excitement infectious and moving at the same time. She prayed that Huw would come out before the various children's fathers because she knew that watching the little ones reunited with their fathers would be too much for her. Rhiannon recalls one little girl who kept asking, 'When will her daddy be coming,? 'She was about five or six, and when the dad came through . . . well, I watched them and my eyes were welling up. When you see homecomings on TV, with kids running to their parent in uniform, that still gets me even after being an army wife for ten years.'

Huw's bag was taking a while to come through, so Rhiannon had to watch three such reunions, the lump in her throat growing at the sight of each one. Then Huw came through. Rhiannon was standing quite far back and she could see her husband looking for her – he'd lost weight and looked tired and thin. They locked eyes and Huw walked over to her. 'We had a little hug and a kiss on the cheek once we were outside,' remembers Rhiannon, 'we're not one for public displays of affection – I was very aware that there were half a dozen of his soldiers on the plane.'

R&R, short for rest and recuperation, is the pivotal midpoint in any tour of duty, the longed-for two weeks off that the men are given during their six long months away. This can be taken as early as six weeks into tour and as late as the very end – meaning you come home two weeks early. Most couples aim for midway, or the second half of the tour – of course, not everyone gets the dates they want but a decent senior officer and welfare team will do their best to make sure the priority requests for R&R are met where possible and that as many of the men as feasible get the dates that work best for them.

When Ed was in Iraq we opted for R&R four months after he went away, feeling that a short stretch at the end was by far the best option. I spent the few weeks before his homecoming in a state of fevered excitement – literally counting the days down – my outfit was meticulously planned, leg wax booked and the days we would have together organised down to the last minute. I knew it would be wonderful and when Ed had to go back to Iraq we would only have just over a month and a half to suffer through before he came home for good.

The homecoming at R&R is very different from the reunion at the end of the tour: R&R is very much a holiday, there is no point trying to get back into a normal routine because they are home for such a short amount of time. Instead the two weeks feels like playing hooky from real life and most wives I know treat it as such. It is, of course, wonderful to see the person you love but it is also very hard, and in a way disruptive, to have them home only to say goodbye again after just fourteen days together and I can confidently say that the end of R&R is in the back of most couples' minds from the moment the soldier first gets home.

I know of one couple who have agreed that the husband should only take R&R at the very end of the tour – effectively bringing his final homecoming forward two weeks and not returning to the front line. This major and his wife prefer to push on through, feeling that a sudden break would be disruptive to him once he's in soldier mode, and also to his wife, who by the time he could take R&R has got used to coping alone. Better for them, and their children, to only have one emotional goodbye and one reunion. Ed has told me stories of soldiers who, traumatised by what they have seen at war, did not want to come home for R&R, not knowing how to be a father and husband again, while realising that they still have to return to the front line. For most soldiers, though, R&R is a welcome interlude: a much-needed break from the relentlessness of tour and a chance to have some time together with their families without having to slot back into the routine of everyday life.

Craig's R&R was allocated at around halfway through the tour but, as luck would have it, the two weeks he would have off coincided with the young couple's first wedding anniversary. In the month before, Donna tried desperately to not get too excited – three-year-old Bradley kept her busy, as he wasn't at school so keeping the youngster occupied was a full-time job. Donna would take her son to the park, meeting with other mums and, while the children played, she couldn't help but let her mind wander to Craig's imminent homecoming, looking forward to spending R&R with the man she loved and thinking about the life she knew would begin once her husband was home for good. Bradley was used to Craig being away but this tour Donna felt her son missed him. 'He did ask about him,' recalls Donna, 'he missed fighting with him and playing football and swimming – that was their thing, going to the Tidworth leisure centre and I told Bradley that dad would be home soon to take him swimming. They got on really well and we didn't tell people that he wasn't his biological father – and nobody would have guessed – in fact people still say now that he looks like Craig. So as well as looking forward to R&R for myself, I knew Craig and Bradley would be so pleased so see one another.'

Elaine was gutted that husband Pete was going to miss her thirtieth birthday – the R&R he'd been allocated was several weeks later – but she hoped it would be a fun weekend regardless. The 2 R Welsh 'wives' exercise', where WAGs get a taste of what their other halves go through while training by camping out for the night on Salisbury Plain, was on and Elaine was looking forward to donning her husband's uniform for an evening of playing soldiers (and drinking wine) with her fellow army wives. After the exercise she was planning a birthday party in the welfare office. It wouldn't be the same without Pete but she was expecting about twenty-five good friends to show up – her mum and her best friend and neighbour Louise were going to help with the buffet of sandwiches, sausage rolls, crisps and dips and there was to be a marquee for the grown-ups and a bouncy castle for the kids to play on. Then, two days before the party, Pete rang home asking Elaine where she would be that weekend. 'I asked him, "Why?"' Elaine remembers,' and he said, "I wasn't going to tell you, but I'm coming home."'

On the Saturday of the party, Elaine and Louise left the wives' exercise early to get ready for the party and also so Elaine could collect Pete from the parade ground at midday. All dressed up in white linen trousers, a peach vest top, white sandals, with her long brown hair left loose, Elaine's stomach was filled with butterflies. Her dad gave her a lift, telling the kids – because they wanted to surprise them with their dad's unexpected return – that they were just going into camp to collect something.

Waiting on the parade square for the bus bringing her husband home, Elaine found she couldn't stop giggling –

like an excited teenager. Then there he was – they shared a hug and a kiss before holding hands and walking to the car. On the way back to the house they dropped Pete by the local park before joining the kids in the garden at home. The children were full of questions about what mum and granddad had been doing in camp. Elaine avoided answering until the side gate to the garden swung open and in walked their dad. 'They saw him and they ran up to him and hugged him,' remembers Elaine with a smile. 'He was in his deserts, all dusty and smelly, but they didn't care – it was lovely – and really sad. We were so relieved he was back, but I think although you can enjoy R&R, I don't think you can relax, because you know they're going back. None the less it was a lovely birthday – he said he was sorry he hadn't had a chance to get me a birthday present, but I said, "That's OK – I'll let you off this time."'

Ed had spent his birthday in Iraq and had been away for it the year before too, training in Canada, so I was determined that during this R&R, just under two months after the actual day, we would celebrate properly. I arranged a surprise party, organising his friends from around the country to be at my mum's house to toast my soldier. We'd had four days together at this point but still it was hard to tear myself from his side on the premise of giving him some one-on-one time with his parents while I went home to prepare things. Nursing a hangover from the night before (a leaving party for a friend heading to Afghanistan) and looking decidedly scruffy, his face lit up as he came into the garden to be met by his closest friends all shouting 'Surprise!' It was a lovely night and after his belated birthday cake candles had been blown out and Happy Birthday sung he stood to thank me for organising it. The truth was, however, that plotting and planning had been a great distraction: knowing we had such a wonderful R&R to look forward to had made the darkest days of separation bearable.

It was the best two weeks; we flitted from London to Bath, from his parents to mine, seeing everyone he wanted, but also making sure we had time for just us – four days in Devon with unseasonably hot September weather were spent pottering about on a boat in the river Dart, eating picnics and enjoying chilled pints outside country pubs. We had a wonderful sense of holiday, of skiving from work and real life. I couldn't stop holding his hand, kissing him, finding it hard to believe, even days into our time together, that it was real, he was really there with me. Of course in the back of both our minds was the fast approaching end of R&R, when he would have to return to Iraq. I selfishly didn't want to be apart from him for even one second and thankfully his mum and dad – old hands at R&R – completely understood. 'We used to tell my mother that I only had a week off when it was two, so we could spend the second week just us together,' confided Ed's father Robin, 'you don't have to share Ed with us.'

Lee's R&R was booked in towards the end of his tour of Iraq – he would be home for two weeks at the end of October, with the tour finishing for good on 4 December. Amanda couldn't wait – it had been a long five months without her husband and despite him having to return to the war zone after the break, R&R felt like the end of a very long road for the couple. Amanda was volunteering full-time for the Help for Heroes at this point; the work was busy and a welcome distraction while Lee was away, but the team in the office fully understood that while Lee was home, her soldier would be getting Amanda's full attention and she would not be coming into work. Amanda's younger brother was staying with her – he was heartbroken after breaking up with the girlfriend he adored and, always thinking of others, Amanda was doing her best to look after him. But uncharacteristically, when Lee returned, all she could think was she didn't want her brother around for Lee's R&R. 'I apologised to Lee,' remembers Amanda, 'and said, "I'm really sorry that my brother's going to be here the whole time." He just told me to not to be selfish, and accept that my brother was hurting and needed some love. He saw things a lot more clearly than I did.'

During R&R, Lee didn't talk about the tour at all except to tell his wife that things were safer out there than they had been. 'He always reassured me that he was all right and safe where he was,' Amanda says, 'but he never told me any details and I preferred to live in blissful ignorance.'

Ed was more talkative – knowing how much I wanted to know, he regaled me with stories of mortar attacks in camp, where the piercing shriek of the alarm was so common that the men would continue whatever they where doing, albeit whilst lying on the floor. Ed showed me comedy snaps of him and colleagues in full body armour lying on the floor with a plate of food in front of them – giving a cheery thumbs-up for the camera. Having been to Iraq myself as a journalist and spent time in British Army base Basra Palace, mortared seventy times the day I was there, Ed knew there was no point pretending to me that he had not had some hairy moments. In fact, given a free rein, Ed seemed to positively revel in telling me his war stories and, having one or two of my own by this point, we were able to compare notes.

It is down to the individual couple, really, to decide how much a husband shares of his experience in a conflict zone, particularly during R&R. Some wives want to know everything and some don't. Many, like Amanda, would rather the frightening details were saved for the end of the tour when their husband is home safe and sound for good (or at least until the next tour). Personally, I feel that it is important, at some point, to talk about what goes on out there otherwise the six-month separation can be lengthened emotionally, the lack of mutual understanding and shared experience unwittingly creating a gap in the relationship. But I completely understand those men who want to protect their wives from the truth of the level of danger they have been in, and those women who want to believe the fib that it is 'quite quiet really', at least until the tour is completely over.

Elaine struggled to fully relax during Pete's leave. 'You can't really enjoy it,' she says. 'He didn't say anything about what he'd seen and done, because he knew I'd be upset when he went back.' The couple spent the two weeks at home in Tidworth. Elaine took one of the weeks off work but they didn't do much; the kids were still at school so they tried to keep things as normal as possible. 'That's my role here, then there's him and I come last,' says Elaine. 'The kids always have to come first.'

Kaz admits that when her husband Brian went back to Afghanistan, she cried more than when he first left. 'Because I knew what he was going back to,' she explains. 'He'd shown photos of where he slept and ate and, oh God, it's just so harrowing to know that's where they're living.' Brian was subdued during his two-week break, not distant, just not quite himself. Kaz knew that in some ways he would almost rather not come home on R&R because as soon as he was settled and they were used to one another, it would be time to pack up his kit and say goodbye all over again. They had a nice time together – pottering around the house, cuddling up while Brian, inevitably wearing his favourite *Rocky* dressing gown, watched the rugby and boxing that Kaz had recorded for him on the Sky box. Kaz loved having him home, but she couldn't shake the feeling of dread that soon she was going to have to say goodbye again.

Even the most mundane tasks on returning home can be loaded with meaning. One item of clothing that Brian brought home for washing had particular significance for him: a pair of blue boxer shorts, full of holes and, quite frankly, disgusting. Holding them outstretched, between finger and thumb, Kaz asked why on earth he had kept such a manky item of clothing. Superstition takes many forms and Brian had decided that it was this item of underwear that was in some way keeping him safe in Afghanistan. 'They're my lucky boxers,' he stated, as if it was obvious, before telling his wife under no circumstance was she to throw them away. Brian had washed them out in camp every day ready to wear the next, and the constant use had taken their toll. 'They were more like a rag than a pair of boxer shorts,' remembers Kaz, 'but I did what I was told and washed them for him to take back out there after R&R.'

The stress of a six-month separation takes a toll on even the strongest of relationships. When Ed returned from Iraq we struggled to find equilibrium. Ed was very much in soldier mode – used to having his barked orders obeyed and also to a world where a good day meant no one being killed. He struggled to be patient with the mundane aspects of everyday life, unable to see that my bad day at work could actually be counted as a bad day. In turn, I had gone from missing him desperately to suddenly having him living in my flat – miserable, and without a doubt a different man from the one who had gone away. We came through it, but it is undoubtedly the case that the constant separations mean you have to work at a relationship perhaps harder than a 'civilian' marriage; and, of course, many army marriages don't survive the constant strain put on them by military life.

Kaz and Brian had been together for five years when they split up. At that time, Kaz knew of four other couples who were going through the same thing. 'It happens quite a lot,' she says. 'As the tours and wars have got worse, marriages have suffered. These tours are make or break and some of them get married, the soldier is twenty-one and the wife is nineteen, and for that girl to come up here and be on her own must be very difficult. Hard enough as an older woman . . .'

Kaz suffers from MS and has been unable to work since moving to Tidworth because she is unable to predict how her health will be from one day to the next. Fifteen years older than Brian, her age has never been an issue for them – or her illness. 'I got MS eleven years ago now, but he knew about it when he married me and the MS never fazed him at all,' Kaz remembers with a smile. 'The only thing I'm really sad about is that I miscarried two babies. He would have loved to have had children and would have been a fantastic father – but after splitting up and getting back together we've said, "If it's not meant to be, it's not meant to be." He's marvellous with Megan – who's not his daughter, but she calls him "Daddy Brian". They get on brilliantly. We just joke that, hopefully, we'll have grandchildren one day. I think our split made me a lot stronger and I'm a different person – more the person that he married. I was very independent then, but I gave up my job because of the MS, so when I came here I had nothing.'

Brian was on a posting in Wales when the couple split up – he had come back from a difficult tour of Iraq where the battalion suffered losses; then he was pall-bearer at the funerals of two colleagues. 'It had a massive effect on him,' Kaz says, 'and he was telling me, "I want to go and live my life. I don't want to be married." I just lost him totally – he was nothing like the man I married. He wouldn't speak about it and he was happy to distance himself totally from this life, from our life. It was a really sad time. The guys all knew each other, although he wasn't close to any of the boys that he buried. I remember going down to Wales before one of the funerals and being at his mother's and he spoke to me in a way he'd never spoken to me before – we don't row and he never talks down to me. I said, "How dare you speak to me like that?" and he responded, "Well, I don't care." I said to his mother, "This is not Brian." She said it was the funerals, and that they'd had a massive impact on him. Looking back, I was pushing him further away because I wasn't being understanding or giving him the space he needed, I was more frightened about losing him myself but at the time I couldn't see that and I was trying to salvage something that couldn't be salvaged at that time.'

The couple got back together for a few months before splitting again. Kaz was hurt and lonely but she never stopped loving her husband so, when Brian called nine months later and said, 'I think I want to try again. I think I made a mistake,' Kaz gave it another go. The couple have learnt from this experience and now Brian does his best to talk about the things he has seen and done and Kaz listens. 'At the time I wanted to try to help him, but he wasn't ready to be helped,' she says. 'When he came home from the Afghan tour, where Chris, a 2 R Welsh soldier was killed, I let him talk – and he did.'

For couples who weather the storm – survive the separation, the anxiety of being the wife of a solider, cope with the inevitable changes in a person who has lived through a traumatic tour – a deeper closeness can develop. It was Ed's tour of Iraq that made me certain I wanted to marry him, and for him to feel the same about me. I knew that if we could survive that we could survive anything. The terrible lows of the goodbyes are balanced out by highs that a 'civvy' couple could rarely experience – a letter or a phone call can mean the world, a reunion provoke teenage butterflies in the longest-married of couples. It is a situation that goes on as long as you are married and they are serving, as Amanda explains, 'You expect and hope that they'll come home, and you know and live with the fear that at any time something could happen that means they won't. You just really hope it doesn't. We've been together twenty years and married eighteen but we're still like teenagers in love and that is due in part to the separations – they really make you appreciate them when they are here.'

Kirsty, a new wife going through her first tour, is finding this to be true already. 'You learn to make every moment precious and that's not just a cliché. You live for the next time, that it's all going to be hunky-dory again and we can have happy family time together again.' As a wife you dread the tours, the separations, but part of you has to accept that the man you love does not feel the same – of course they miss you and don't want to be apart, but at the same time they want to do the job they are trained for and that, inevitably, takes them away from you. Mandy explains, 'It is who he is. It's what he is – what's made him who he is today, and I love him more today than when we got married; him doing what he does makes him the person I love and I wouldn't have him any other way, because I know he wouldn't be happy. For me he's dependable, and I see him as dependable for other people as well. I just have to share him with the army.'

It is a thought that is echoed by Kaz, 'For Brian, this is what he enjoys. I hate the tours but it's what Brian joined the army for. He loves the tours. At first I used to wonder, "Why do they want to go? Why are they so happy to go on these tours when they're supposed to be so in love with you?" But you come to realise that that is their other love and it doesn't distract from the love they have for you. It's what they enjoy doing, and it's what Brian was doing before he met me. I think his heart and soul have always been in his job – and though I know he loves me, it's his job.'

Driving Ed back to Brize Norton at the end of R&R was a miserable experience. We both sat in silence, hating the fact that we were having to say goodbye again. We'd got lucky; his original flight had been delayed, giving us an unexpected bonus day together, which we had spent cuddled up on my mother's sofa watching films. But when it came to it, the goodbye was not as hard as I'd feared and certainly much less painful than when he left originally – we knew we were near the end and Iraq was no longer an unknown entity – we had both been there and survived so to me it felt less scary. Of course this is not the case for all wives: for Kaz, sending Brian back to the place he had seen a colleague killed was agonising and I know many women find it hard to say goodbye for a second time when they understand better the danger their husband is facing.

Delays meant Rhiannon and Huw also had an extra day together. It had been a lovely break – they went up to London for a couple of days – but in the main, Huw had just wanted to chill out at home. The timing for Huw's R&R wasn't ideal, as Rhiannon had her final chartered tax adviser exams to prepare for, so the first four days of his leave she spent studying and then taking the exams. Huw took the opportunity to visit his family alone. It was a good R&R, but

Huw was keen to get back by the end of it. 'He didn't want to miss stuff happening out there,' explains Rhiannon. 'I wasn't worried – I went back to Brize to drop him off, and it was nice to know we were halfway through. You felt you were on your way.'

CHAPTER 6

'Every Time It's On The News, You Pray That It's Somebody You Don't Know'

I t became nothing short of an addiction – easily distracted from work and social life, I found myself constantly clicking on the BBC, Sky and the Ministry of Defence news websites – a quick scan was normally all I'd need, but boy did I need it. I would get anxious if I was away from the internet or somewhere my phone didn't have reception. Working as a journalist I suppose it was inevitable that I would go down this route of needing to know *everything* while Ed was in Iraq but even I was surprised by the ferocity of my appetite for information about the conflict zone, the minutiae of daily life out there and, of course, the bad news. Ed wasn't much help – even when he called he was limited as to what he could tell me, security risks meaning that discussing specifics on a satellite phone was a definite no. So instead I devoured every news item I could, reading articles in newspapers that before would have warranted little more than a cursory glance and I became so reliant on the MOD news website that it was always open somewhere on my computer – I knew that if someone was killed this would be the first place the terrible news would be posted.

You don't need to be a journalist to have unlimited access to information: twenty-four-hour news stations and the web mean that with a click of the button you can get update bulletins immediately about what is happening out in Afghanistan and, most importantly, learn if there have been any fatalities. It must have been a very different tour experience for army wives of the past when not only were post and letters infrequent but, without the internet, it was much harder to find out what was going on in the part of the world where their husbands were stationed.

I used to dread and look forward to the news in equal measure, breathing a sigh of relief after the headlines had been announced and there was no report of anyone being killed, or that British troops were gearing up for a big offensive. Selfishly, I didn't have much interest in any other headlines – I was so wrapped up in my own worried world that I didn't have the emotional energy to think about other tragedies or events around the globe, but I would watch it all regardless in case at the end there was some small bit of information about Iraq. The best would be a report including (safe) footage of Iraq. I loved seeing a small glimpse of the world Ed was living in and the images of camps in a dusty desert landscape, of helicopters and men in uniform brought his letters to me to life. Our phone conversations, letters, the MOD website and the news helped me imagine what Ed's days were like and I found this a huge comfort.

Not everyone is like me. In fact many wives go completely the opposite way and don't want to know anything, avoiding the news and pretending as much as possible that their loved one is just away training rather than in a war zone. Julie always used to steer clear of the news but when her husband Dai was last away, she couldn't stop her son from switching on the TV relentlessly to try and find out what was happening. 'As the kids get older it gets a lot harder,' Julie says, 'My youngest one was about nine and he was addicted to the news but I never watched it, I didn't want to know – what I didn't know didn't hurt me, but my boy just wanted to watch what was going on. I didn't agree with it but I couldn't ruddy well stop him – his dad was out in Iraq and he just wanted to know that his dad was all right.' Dereynn, like Julie, finds that now her children are older she can't protect them from the headlines, 'When Taff is away I sometimes wish my kids were a lot younger,' she explains, 'because then you can say, "Don't worry, dad's fine," and reassure them. But as they get older they watch the news and they know – but I just have to tell them that if something had happened to him, we'd have been the first port of call.'

Elaine's two children are also now at the age when their mum can't hide from them what is going on. They are used to dad being away but during this most recent tour, able now to watch the news and listen with understanding to grown-up conversations, Elaine realised quite how much this greater knowledge was affecting them. 'I was talking about Pete to our son and I said, "When your dad comes back," and he asked me, "Why do you keep saying 'when'?" I said, "Because he'll be back soon." And he said, "You should say, 'If he ever comes back,'" I was shocked, sad, but I told him, "Of course he's going to come back". It made me realise that they had it in the back of their minds as well, that they might not see him again.'

From the moment her son James left for Afghanistan, Sarah was addicted to the news; she would listen to the radio in her car and at work, and at home the television was permanently on in the corner of her living room. Like me, Sarah wanted to know as much as possible so, before James deployed, she sat and watched the TV documentary series *Ross Kemp in Afghanistan*, to try and understand what her eldest son would be facing. Her family didn't think it was a good idea but Sarah wanted to know and knew her son would not tell her what he would be going through. 'I tried to explain to them,' Sarah says. 'I told them – "I need to know what he's dealing with. I want to be able to help if I need to – so I want some idea, however small, of what's going to go on." But I don't think they got it. I'm better like that – if I don't know, I will make it up in my head and, trust me, what I imagine will be far worse than the reality. I was obsessed with watching the news and reading the papers – thankfully, the people at work were very supportive and very good. I've got a picture on my desk of James, and everybody knew he was going, and they were telling me that "He'd be fine, though it must be awful", so that's what I kept telling myself – '"He'll be fine, he'll be fine."'

*

One of the hardest things to deal with is when well-meaning people ask if you have heard the news that someone has been killed. More often than not, I had seen the news but the constant reminder from people was emotionally wearing. The only reassurance for anxious loved ones, watching the news religiously, is that if you hear about a death on the news it won't be the person you care about because of a failsafe system which is in place to ensure that, until the next of kin has been informed, no news about a death or injury is leaked.

Out in Afghanistan, communications are put on OP MINIMISE, meaning that no calls can be made or emails sent back to the UK. This is to ensure that someone doesn't mention the incident to the person they are calling and thus launching, unwontedly, a spread of wildfire rumours culminating in a family hearing the most terrible news from a friend or neighbour. The sad side-effect is that so often a weekly call home is delayed or missed because the phones out in Afghanistan are so frequently on OP MINIMISE status, which illustrates clearly the high number of incidents when someone is killed or seriously injured (something which is not reported in the press).

When Ed was away and I was expecting a call from him which didn't come I would always hold my breath with dread for the inevitable news story would follow that. and in my own time in Afghanistan, of the four days I spent in Camp Bastion there was only one day I was able to call or email, despite no one being killed when I was there – the number of people seriously injured meant OP MINIMISE was on daily.

Despite all these precautions, there is always a risk that in a close-knit community like Tidworth someone somewhere will unintentionally pass on a piece of information – of the less serious, but still upsetting, kind. One day, about two months into her husband Mark's tour, Simone popped out to the local Spar shop to buy her daily newspaper. She bumped into another wife while she was paying and instead of the usual pleasantries the wife said, 'Is Mark OK?' Simone responded, 'Yes, as far as I know.' Simone remembers, 'She said, "Oh, good," and looked awkward. For some reason something in me just clicked and I knew something was wrong; why had she asked me? We weren't close friends and she wasn't just inquiring after my husband, it was more than that.'

Simone rushed home and was on tenterhooks waiting for Mark to call. 'When he phoned as he'd promised later that day, I said, "Mark, I've just heard something in the Spar. I need to know if something has happened." He said, "Who the hell said something to you? Don't panic – I'm absolutely fine. I made the decision not to tell you, because I know how worried you are about me, but the Warrior (tank) hit a roadside bomb and I've had to have treatment for my eyes and a burn on my leg." He said there was just a hole in the bottom of the Warrior. I think there must have been a flame because he lost his eyelashes and eyebrows, and there was a big hole in his trousers and he burned his leg. He didn't go into loads of details – but he said he was OK. I gave him a piece of my mind for not telling me, and he apologised – and I understood why he hadn't. He was hoping that the other guys there wouldn't tell their wives either. They'd made that decision between them – because if they were OK there was no point in worrying us.'

All members of the armed forces fill out a form before they deploy, ensuring that the welfare team have the right names and contact details of whom the serving member would want to be contacted should something happen to them. Being the next of kin doesn't automatically mean you will be the first person told; I know of wives who have opted to put their in-laws down, not wanting to be told the worst news imaginable when they were on their own. Once the official people within the battalion have been informed of the incident, two elected individuals will be sent to the next of kin's house to tell them. They will then stay with the person, supporting and helping in any way they can, for as long as necessary.

I didn't want to be Ed's next of kin when he deployed to Iraq, so it was as it had always been; he left his parents as both next of kin and the people to go to should something happen. At that stage when I was 'just' a girlfriend, even talking about the form was something I couldn't bear – and the idea, should he be killed, of having the responsibility of informing others, was unthinkable. In hindsight it was a bad idea because whenever a story came on the news that a soldier had been killed in Iraq, I would panic it was Ed, that his parents had been told but for some reason not got hold of me. I had to fight the urge to ring his father breathless with worry, knowing in my heart of hearts that of course they would have been in touch. The other side effect of this arrangement was that every time my mobile rang showing the caller display to be my husband's parents' home number, I would freeze with horror and have to will myself to answer, praying that it was just Robin or Sarah calling for a catch-up, which, thank God, it always was.

Far worse than dreading a phone call is the dread of an unexpected knock on the door; a knock feared by any person whose loved one is in a conflict zone and knows that it is their home which the informing officers will come to first. The older Daffodil Girls tell me that the fear of this knock never leaves you. Amanda explains, 'I shouted at Meg the other night; one of her friends had knocked on the door quite late, and I could feel my stomach drop instantly. I said, "Who's that – who's there?" She rushed to the door and it was one of her friends – and I said, "Megan, you need to tell your friends they're not to knock on the door this late at night." It was only about half-past nine. She said I was totally over-reacting – which I was, but my first thought was, "Oh my God!" It's easier not to watch the news, not to have the door knocked on, or the phone ringing late and just be ignorant.'

Kaz remembers a knock at the door when Brian was on tour and she wasn't expecting any visitors; it was in the evening and the bang on the door made her heart leap into her mouth. The person outside thumped again and Kaz leapt up to answer, to find a policeman standing on her doorstep. 'They'd been burgled next door and he wanted to know if I'd heard anything,' she recalls. 'It was such a relief.'

Elaine says she thinks about 'the knock' every day that her husband is away, even though she knows there is nothing she could do about it should it actually come. Elaine is a news watcher, knowing that she won't find out information in any other way – husband Pete begs her to not watch it and even though she knows he is right, that watching it undoubtedly makes her worry more, she can't help herself. 'One night I dreamt he was killed,' she tells me. 'It plays on your mind that often – you expect it all the time. It was a really vivid dream, I remember being at his funeral, it was so vivid it took me a moment when I woke up to realise it wasn't true.' For Elaine, and many of the Daffodil Girls, the hard thing about the tour is not the separation, as army wives they are used to that. The real strain comes from the constant fear, the pressure of knowing their husband is somewhere where the worst could, and does, happen.

Dereynn struggles to sleep when Taff is away; bedtime is always the point that she can't quash the dark imaginings and she tortures herself thinking about the knock at the door. Even when she eventually does drop off to sleep, it is a cautious sleep, one that you never allow yourself to fall into too deeply. Bedtimes are the worst for Simone as well; she lies there convinced the doorbell is going to ring, that someone is going to come and tell her the news she dreads. In her head she pictures it over and over, imagining herself going downstairs, opening the door and the officers asking her to identify herself before saying, 'I am sorry to tell you but . . .'. She then goes on to imagine calling his family and telling them – on really bad nights she even finds herself unwittingly thinking about husband Mark's funeral, hot tears rolling down her face as she plans the thing she dread most in the world. Despite taking herbal remedies to help her sleep nothing works and Simone can just lie there awake into the early hours

'I was doing that nearly every single night,' Simone says. 'Every morning I'd wake up and think, "It didn't happen again," and feel relieved and promise myself that the next night I wouldn't torture myself thinking about it but I couldn't help myself. After a few months I started relaxing and thinking, "If it's going to happen, it's going to happen – no matter if I sit here every single night, tormenting myself." Maybe I did it because it felt that if I was imagining the worst, suffering through it, then it couldn't happen for real and I was protecting him.'

It is a feeling I can identify with – when Ed was away I lived in a permanent sense of anxiety, bad dreams were a norm and I could drive myself to tears imagining the worse. I woke in the early hours of most mornings, forgetting, for a blissful minute or two, to worry before I remembered where he was. But if I am honest I didn't want to stop worrying – when someone you love is fighting in a war zone you want to worry about them, you want to feel anxious and when, in a brief moment of fun with friends, you forget, well, then you can feel guilty. It is as though your worry, your constant thoughts, will protect the person you are missing, shield them from the bombs and bullets and bring them home safely, and if you forget to think about them – even for a few minutes of a day – you are letting them down, you are putting them at risk.

For Kirsty, Amanda and Sian there is an added dimension to the worry because they work for a charity that helps wounded military personnel. There is no hope of burying your head in the sand, ignoring the realities of war, when your working day is spent helping to raise money which is to improve the lives of those grievously wounded in the very place where your husband is currently serving. The walls of their office are filled with photos of young men with missing limbs, and every other phone call from supporters is filled with stories of loss and heroism.

Kirsty explains, 'I get people who tell me they're doing runs and fund-raising in memory of someone who died or because someone they love has been injured. The numbers of injured are not published on the news but, through Help for Heroes, I have realised it is a lot. It is more likely that Ben will be injured rather than killed but it has got to the point that I don't hold much value to his limbs any more – I see how young men have overcome the most appalling of injuries, some living full lives after losing three limbs, so I just want Ben to come home to me; I can't think about any other option. Before he left we were looking at his PAX insurance, which is injury and life insurance for soldiers, and there was something about what you get if you lose different parts of your body – even if you hurt your little finger you get a few thousand. I was saying, "Well you don't need a little finger," It was tickling us in the end – well, you've got to find something to laugh about, haven't you?'

But for all her bravado the fear of the knock on the door is something Kirsty is struggling with. 'The other night I was in bed and I was convinced that I heard knocking on the door – and my doorbell doesn't work,' she says. 'It was in the middle of the night; I could hear about five knocks in a row, and I thought, "Oh my God . . ." I was glued to my bed, but it was nothing. I'm worried that someone will show up at my house, not constantly worried, but in the nights it hits me, especially when it's all dark. Even if they're "just" injured, they come and knock on your door. I can pretty much take my mind completely away from it in the day. Missing him isn't the problem for me – I'm used to pining after him, to be honest, but it is the panic of it all – if something happened – it's constantly there.'

That sense of relief is one that goes hand in hand with the anxiety experienced by every army wife whose husband is away fighting in a war zone, relief when the knock at the door turns out to be a tradesman or neighbour, relief when you get through any other day, and night, without the most terrible of news being brought to your doorstep, relief as the weeks pass that, so far, it hasn't happened to you.

But of course it does happen and when the news comes through that someone has been killed and it is not 'your' person – there is still a terrible sense of grief coupled with relief, which in turn makes you feel guilty for being relieved because the news of a death means that somebody else's husband, somebody else's son, somebody else's father will not be coming home.

A death affects the wives' community in a way that it is difficult for those outside to understand: "It's our reality," explains Amanda. "Civilian people find it easier to remove themselves from it, and can see it as 'just' another British soldier, because they don't know the depth behind it. Every time it's on the news that somebody has been killed in action, you always pray that it's somebody you don't know. Then you feel selfish and guilty as well – and sorry that some poor bugger's family is going through that heartache. It's a mixture of everything – you feel really anxious and then there's a news story on and you just wonder if it's somebody very close to you and when you learn that is isn't there's a sad mixture between happiness and feeling extremely guilty that some family is having to cope with losing a loved one. We're all guilty of removing ourselves from the situation because we have to protect ourselves as well."

When Mark first went away Simone would panic every time she heard something on the news about a soldier being killed. Mark promised faithfully that the system worked so if she heard it on the news it wouldn't be him. But even so her heart would flutter nervously until Mark was able to call her and she could hear his voice. Even when the soldier was not from the same battalion as Mark, Simone felt physically sick: 'First of all I would think of the family – that poor family had got to be told that this person had died.' Simone remembers, 'You think "Thank God it isn't Mark," which is selfish, but at the time you're so upset about the person it's happened to. All you want to do is speak to your husband, because it's such a horrible thing to happen, you want to speak to the person you love and in the back of your mind is the fact that there is a wife or mother out there who will never get to speak to the person they love again.

'It is terrible when any soldier dies,' says Dereynn. 'Even if they are not from the battalion we are linked because you are part of the same community, the army community. It is even worse if the news comes that someone from the battalion has been killed, you see you'll most likely know them then, you hear their name and then you picture their face. It's hard to imagine how that family's going to react – to get that knock at the door. I wouldn't know where to start – if it happened here. My heart goes out to them.'

CHAPTER 7

'He's Dead, Isn't He?'

'I heard it first on the news, the same as everyone else, that a soldier from The 2nd Battalion The Royal Welsh had been killed, but they didn't release any names. Then just after that, I had a call from the welfare office and I'd asked if the man killed was married – not that it makes any difference, but I knew there might have been a wife out there that needed some support. I was told he was married, and that he had a little boy . . .' Amanda

It was about half-past five in the morning when the phone rang. Rhiannon and Huw sat up in bed and looked at one another, both knowing instantly – a call that time in the morning is never going to be good news. As Huw was duty field officer, the couple knew almost certainly that something must have happened to one of the 2 Royal

Welsh soldiers currently serving in Afghanistan. Huw leapt out of bed and took the phone out of the bedroom to have the conversation in private. When he came back into the room he started to get dressed. 'Is it bad?' Rhiannon asked her husband. 'Yes,' came the short reply. He told his wife that someone had been killed and that he was going to inform the wife, and then left. 'You never think it's going to happen,' Rhiannon says. 'There was the married man who died in Iraq, but we weren't with the battalion then, so it had never happened during our time. There was the shock that that had happened and I was terrified for Huw – I thought that he's got to do this, and he's going to be that person that brings someone's nightmare to reality, and I was so worried for him.'

Rhiannon knew that her husband would do the best job he could in the worst possible of circumstances and from the moment he left there was nothing for her to do but wait for his return. She couldn't settle or do anything – she hated not knowing what was happening but at the same time felt terrible that she knew anything at all. 'I felt it was wrong that I knew someone had died before his wife did, even though I didn't even know the soldier's name,' she says. 'I knew that Huw was going to tell the wife – but I knew first, and I shouldn't have done. I was just waiting, ready to support Huw when he got back because I knew that he was going to need a big hug. What he was going through was nothing to the devastation he's just laid on this family, but it was my job to listen to him.'

When Huw finally came home, much later that morning, he was shell-shocked; he walked in the door in his suit and the couple sat on the sofa in the lounge and he told his wife step by step what had happened, from going into the office, making the decision who was going to go, what they were going to wear and do. Rhiannon again struggled with the idea that there were people sitting talking about it before the wife knew, but understood that it had to be done this way. Huw told her about arriving at the widow's house, and going up the stairs. Rhiannon's eyes pricked with unshed tears as her husband described the past few terrible hours. The phone rang relentlessly all day, Huw called a few key people to let them know what was going on and as word spread, people called Huw to offer their support, aware that telling the family is one of the hardest things a soldier can ever be asked to do – the one task you are trained for that you hope and pray you will never have to complete.

'That was a very long day,' remembers Rhiannon. 'It really proves what a network the regiment is, because the phone didn't stop ringing all weekend. The soldier killed was called Chris and he was only twenty-two; his father and grandfather had served with the battalion so everyone knew him in one way or another. Many of the calls were fellow officers ringing to offer support to Huw; it was as if by supporting him, they were supporting that family and wife, because they knew they couldn't ring them yet, you have to step away and then it's about the family being together and somehow getting through that day. How do you get through that day? I can't imagine.'

The married soldier who died in Iraq, and who Rhiannon had referred to, was Craig. It had been eleven days before Craig's R&R and Craig's little sister, twelve-year-old Beccy, was staying with Donna. It was a warm English summer's day and Donna was starting to let herself get excited about her husband's homecoming. The day before, Craig had called with more time than normal to talk to his wife but, busy with Beccy and Bradley, it was Donna who had to cut the conversation short. The couple spoke long enough for Craig to tell his wife that things were improving out there, as always Donna rang her mother-in-law to pass on the news. 'By the sounds of it, it's gone quite quiet now – nobody's been hurt or injured in so long,' Donna had told her. 'We'll be all right now. He'll be home shortly.'

That night, at half-past eleven, Donna was lying in bed, unable to sleep. She heard a knock at the door. She knew most of her friends were away that week and that, anyway, they wouldn't call on her at such a late hour. She remembers knowing instantly that there was only one reason why someone would be knocking on her door at this time. She got out of bed, opened the window and looked out – on the doorstep was a man she didn't recognise, dressed in uniform. 'Are you Mrs Barber?' he asked and Donna responded, 'Yes.' He said, 'Can you come down?' Donna's heart was in her mouth and she started to shake – she just knew. Beccy and Bradley were fast asleep, so she went downstairs alone, opened the door and said, 'He's dead, isn't he?' The officer asked to come inside and sit down. They went into the house and sat in the sitting room then, confirming what she had known since she first heard the knock at the door, the visiting officer said, 'I'm sorry to tell you, but your husband's been killed in action.'

'At the time I just gasped,' says Donna. 'I was shocked and I wanted to cry, to shout, to scream – everything all at once. I really didn't know what I was meant to do – how to react. I'm not sure what he said after that.'

The visiting officer offered to make Donna a cup of tea but she stood up to do it herself, hoping the mundane task would occupy her mind, if even just for a moment. She needed to call Craig's mum – before Craig left they had agreed as a family that Craig's grandparents (Nan and Bampy) and Donna would be the ones who were notified but Donna had promised to ring his mum, Cheryl, immediately – never, of course, imagining she would ever have need to do so. When the moment came Donna found she just couldn't do it. 'Do you mind talking to her?' she said, passing the phone to the visiting officer. Normally the officers are not allowed to tell people over the phone, but because Donna asked him, telling him that she had promised to phone to tell Cheryl, he agreed. 'I don't think he needed to tell her,' remembers Donna, 'because she knew – she saw my number come up and heard a man's voice, that late at night; she said she knew as soon as she heard the phone ringing.'

Cheryl said she would drive to Tidworth from her home in Wales immediately and the women agreed that Donna should leave the children sleeping until Cheryl got there.

Donna went to make another cup of tea, the thought 'Craig's dead, Craig's dead' repeating endlessly in her mind – but she didn't really believe it, it seemed so unreal. 'I had never ever had to deal with anything near as bad as that before,' says Donna. 'It was confusing and I didn't know how I should be acting or what I should be saying.'

At this point a second visiting officer arrived, and Donna joined the two men in the sitting room clutching the mug of tea so tightly that the hot liquid turned her palm red. She lit a cigarette. 'We were chatting about quite normal stuff, taking my mind off it,' says Donna. 'It seemed like a sort of joke – this can't really be happening. Even though two people have come to tell you, how can you believe them when you haven't any evidence? They couldn't tell me how he'd died, or what time he'd died. I just couldn't believe it.'

Two weeks previously, a mate of Craig's had been home on R&R and had dropped off a letter for Donna; it was for her to open in the event of Craig's death. Soldiers are quite often advised to write these before a tour but Donna had no idea why Craig had decided to write his halfway through and send it. 'Hopefully, when I get back, we'll read it together,' Craig had cheerily said on the phone but even at the time Donna felt it was tempting fate. Remembering the letter, Donna decided she wanted to be on her own and asked the visiting officers to leave, telling them, 'I'm going to be all right, you know. I'm not going to do anything stupid. I just want to be by myself.'

Reluctantly they left; they wanted to stay until Cheryl arrived but Donna's mind was made up. She sat down on her own and opened the letter. It started, 'If you're reading this, then I've gone to heaven . . .' Donna stopped and went upstairs to lie on the bed. 'I was curled up with this letter trying to make sense of it all,' she remembers. 'It doesn't seem real, because somebody could tell you anything. I just wanted them to be lying, however horrific that would be.'

In the letter Craig told his young wife how much he loved her and son Bradley, how much he would miss them both, that Donna was the love of his life. He wrote that he would always love them but that Donna must go on with her life, re-marry and have more children. He wrote that he wanted her to be happy and she mustn't feel guilty when she moved on with her life.

'I don't think I'd cried at all at that point – I was just trying to make sense of it. In that split second, when that man said that Craig had died, my whole life had come crumbling down. I can't describe how horrific it was.'

At half-past three Cheryl arrived – Donna can't remember what they said or did in those first few painful moments. She remembers giving Cheryl the letter from her son to read, and remembers Cheryl crying uncontrollably. But then it was down to business: Cheryl asked Donna what she wanted – to stay in Tidworth, go to her parents in Catterick or go down to Craig's childhood home in Wales? 'I didn't want to stay in the house anymore,' Donna remembers. 'As far as I was concerned, that house wasn't ours any more so I asked Cheryl to take me back to Wales.' The two women started to collect together everything Bradley and Donna would need for the foreseeable future, then at 6 am Bradley woke up and Cheryl went upstairs to wake Beccy and tell her that her beloved brother was dead. 'That poor girl,' Donna remembers thinking, as she listened to Cheryl walk upstairs, 'she is sleeping now and doesn't know anything about this. Her life is normal – but in a split second her life is going to completely change and fall apart.'

Beccy's screams filled the small house and, finally, Donna was able to cry. 'Hearing it was awful,' recalls Donna. 'She could show her feelings by screaming, whereas I was just quiet and dazed.' Donna and Cheryl decided not to tell Bradley anything at this point, it was so early and he was so little they didn't think he would understand. Donna made an effort to control her emotions in front of the little boy, brightly telling him that they were going to Wales for a visit. The two women loaded up the car and Donna sat in the back with an inconsolable Beccy and Bradley, who promptly went back to sleep. Cheryl's partner was driving and Donna was sitting behind him with her forehead leaning against the window, staring sightlessly out at the gathering dawn, tears sliding silently down her face. 'I must have done that all the way down,' she recalls. 'I was in my own world, thinking about it all, going through memories.'

The last phone call Sarah had from her son James had come early on a Friday evening. James was on great form and the line was the clearest it had been all tour. Sarah was thrilled to hear from her son and even more pleased when he told her that R&R had been set and he would be home in just ten days. James had just come in from guard duty and told his mum he was hungry; she asked him what food he wanted her to get in for R&R but all the young soldier said he fancied was a Burger King. He was upbeat, tired but OK, happy that the phones were up and running. The internet had just starting working in camp – he was looking forward to getting in touch with his friends. Sarah told him that his sister hadn't been very well and suggested he called her which he promised he would and that was it – James said he would try and call before R&R to let her know timings, and then he went.

The next day Sarah woke feeling happier than she had all tour – all she could think was, 'He's coming home in ten days.' Everyone she saw that day noticed the change in her and commented that she seemed much better in herself, and she was suddenly, with the end in sight she forgot to be worried and instead just focused on those ten short days she had to get through till her beloved son would be safely home – for two wonderful weeks.

On the Sunday morning Sarah and her youngest son Josh were up early. Josh had basketball training, so at 7.45 she was in the kitchen getting breakfast, organising and yelling upstairs to her son that he was going to be late, to please hurry up. Josh joined her in the kitchen, grabbing a piece of toast and there was a knock at the door. Sarah felt the colour drain from her face, her stomach clenched in fear and she grabbed the kitchen counter to steady herself. 'It can't be,' she half-whispered. Looking down the corridor to the front door she could see a dark suited figure through the frosted glass; Josh stood frozen, silent. Instead of going to the door she walked down the corridor and turned right into the sitting room so she could look out of the window. Behind the suited man she had seen through the glass front door was a man in uniform, a soldier. 'I just fell apart,' remember Sarah. 'I don't even know the name of the soldier but I can see his face. I'll never forget his face.'

Somehow she made it to the front door and opened it. The first man checked her name and asked if she was James's mother; in the kitchen, Josh started to cry. Sarah doesn't really remember much of what happened next, the men told her that James had been killed in action while driving his Warrior but Sarah kept repeating, 'No – he's coming home in ten days.' They asked who they should call and Sarah said her brother, Andrew, who only lived ten minutes away, but she couldn't remember her brother's number and kept repeating it wrongly, until eventually one of the notifying officers took the phone from Sarah's hand and went through it to find the number.

'I couldn't think of anything but the phone call I'd had,' says Sarah. 'I kept thinking that they'd got it wrong, because he'd said he was coming home. You're aware of the danger but you hope and pray it's not going to be your soldier – your boy. Not that you want it to be anyone else's but when it is you, you just can't believe it.'

After that the day seemed endless; she was told an officer from the battalion would be coming to see them and answer as many questions as they were able, so the day tuned into a waiting game. Endless cups of tea were made, Sarah's brother started telling the people who needed to be told – family and James's close group of friends – James's name was going to be released to the media later that day, so they wanted to make sure that the people who mattered heard it from the family first. One of James's best friends was called and he told the rest of the old gang; people came to see Sarah but she doesn't really remember whom. Andrew then called the boyfriend of Sarah's eldest child, Emma; who then had to tell Emma that her baby brother was never coming home. The couple, based in Nottingham, immediately got in the car for the long drive back to Wales.

Finally, the visiting officer from 2 Royal Welsh arrived but Sarah, in her rage and grief, struggled to get on with him. 'Unfortunately for him, it was the first time he'd been put in this situation,' remembers Sarah, 'and as much as it was hard for him, I think families need to have someone who's strong. There were times when I thought I was going to make him cry and I was very aware of him being so timid. All I had in my mind on the afternoon of that day was that James said he was hungry and that he wanted a Burger King, and I remember yelling at him at one point, "Why was my child hungry?" '

Gradually more information came though and Sarah learned how her son had died: James had head and leg injuries but it was an aortic tear which had killed him. 'When they were putting James on to the helicopter, everybody thought he was coming back, he would be OK, because, even though he was unconscious, outwardly he looked as though he just had injuries which were repairable. But they weren't aware of what was going on internally,' Sarah explains. 'They found out in the field hospital in Bastion and he died there.'

After the death of one of their own, the whole battalion goes into mourning. Even if the individual is not someone you know personally, the community is undoubtedly shattered by the loss. The welfare team are pivotal at this time – helping the bereaved and ensuring that all members of the 2R Welsh family are given the opportunity to pay their respects, to mourn their loss. As wife of the welfare officer, Clare has an important role to play in supporting him during this time, as well as ensuring the wider wives' community is being looked after.

'The guys we lost during the first tour we were around were single soldiers,' Clare says, 'so we had no wives, from my point of view. I was thinking, "Thank God he wasn't married." But he still had parents, a loving family and Mo spent time with them. Although he's not the notifying officer, he's the connection between the battalion and the families. We supported one another – but it's hard getting Mo to talk, as he knows he has to be strong.'

Sarah had been worried about her son's welfare out in Afghanistan, and had called on a number of occasions to voice her concerns. 'It was almost like she knew,' Clare remembers, 'and after he died it was hard for Mo, because the last thing Mo had said to her before was, "Your son's in safe hands."' Sarah requested a visit from Mo and the welfare officer went to Wales and spent the day with her. 'She was honestly going through hell,' Clare tells me, starting to cry. 'Hating the army, hating Mo, so angry. She said to Mo, "You don't know what it's like for a child to die," and he said, "Yes, I do," because we had a baby daughter die ten months before – she was stillborn. I decided then that maybe that was the reason why our daughter Gemma had to die, because our loss and grief, well it made us understand what people go through, when you lose a child. After that they got on fine, because she knew that Mo could understand, in some small way, what she was going though. Sarah's lovely and now wants to do everything she can to help the army charities – I'm sure there are many other families who do exactly the same. I hope people appreciate that they've gone through pain and this is their way of easing that, by helping others and giving a lasting legacy.'

Clare is not the only wife to be involved because of her husband's status; as wife of the company commander, Rhiannon was also informed when anything happened out in Afghanistan. Less than a month after Huw had left to go on tour, Rhiannon was working at her desk when her mobile phone rang. The number was withheld and although Rhiannon knew, logically, she would never be told over the phone if something terrible were to happen to Huw, her first thought was that it had – her heart started to race. She half-ran away from her desk out to where the office loos and tea-making area were, and answered the phone there. It was Mo, and Rhiannon began to shake as he told her there had been an incident.

Rhiannon hadn't realised that, as company com-mander's wife, she would be kept well informed when something happened. Her heart stopped as she thought 'Why is he ringing me? What has happened to Huw?' Mo was reassuringly matter-of-fact and told her that Huw was fine but that two of his soldiers had been injured – one seriously and one they thought would be OK. The wounded men had been taken back to Camp Bastion and were being flown to Selly Oak Hospital in Birmingham as soon as possible. Mo told Rhiannon that OP MINIMISE would be on, so she would be unlikely to hear from her husband. He promised to keep Rhiannon informed, before saying goodbye.

Rhiannon was shaken and it took her a while to calm down. Someone made her a cup of tea – her co-workers realising, perhaps for the first time, the terrible reality of what her husband was doing. Someone suggested she go home but Rhiannon was determined to get back to work. 'I was a bit shocked for a while,' she remembers, 'the surprise of him ringing me – but I could get back to work, you have to. It wasn't my husband or son who was hurt. I get irritated with people if some distant relative's ill and they have to take the afternoon off. I can't be dealing with all that crap – so I pulled myself together.'

Mo rang Rhiannon that weekend to tell her that, once back in the UK, the seriously wounded soldier had died*. 'I was prepared by that point,' remembers Rhiannon. 'The padre had warned me and I knew it was serious – it wasn't looking good. I was upset – you're worried for the family: I

---

*This soldier who had died was Private Richard Hunt, he was 21 and from Abergavenny in Wales. He was mortally wounded as a result of an explosion while on a vehicle patrol near Musa Qaleh in Helmand province on the morning of 13 August 2009. Richard joined the army in October 2007, just 22 months before his death. At the time, Rhiannon's husband Huw said:

"Richard was a fine soldier; fit, professional and extremely brave. He had huge potential and was at the peak of his game, having just completed an arduous and demanding sniper course. It was typical of him to volunteer to drive a Warrior when the need arose. Despite the danger he threw himself at the task with the boundless enthusiasm and selfless commitment which was his hallmark – he set an example for us all. We have lost a man of great courage and skill, and it has wounded us deeply. Our thoughts and prayers are with his family."

wanted to write to his mum and I did the next day. He wasn't married, he was only about twenty-one – but he had a girlfriend.' The girlfriend's name hit home, reminding her how easily the circumstances could have been the other way round, 'She was called Rhiannon as well.'

Donna bought anything that had any mention of Craig in it; it was strange to see her husband's smiling face plastered all over the national papers. Bradley used to get all the papers, those with his daddy's pictures in, put them all over the floor and roll around all over them. He'd tell anyone who was there proudly, 'This is my daddy.' The three-year-old didn't really understand that daddy was dead, what that meant. Used to Craig being away, Bradley took his dad's continuing absence in his stride, spending most of his time playing with his granny's neighbours' kids out in the garden.

Donna had stayed in Wales, not returning to Tidworth or wanting to visit her family home up in Catterick where she and Craig had first met. She wanted to feel close to Craig and here in the village he grew up in, surrounded by the hills he used to walk on, his favourite local pub and all of his family, she felt most at home, closest to him. She told the welfare team where she was and they kept in close contact, regularly sending a visiting officer to see her.

During the next couple of weeks the young wife was bombarded with information and Craig's death was constantly in the papers. 'We read for the first time, in *The Times*, exactly what had happened that day,' she recalls, 'because someone was out there reporting, and had written about

Craig. We went to the shop as we did every morning, to see if there was anything in the paper about him, and there was a whole news feature about the night he died. Whether it was all true or not, I don't know. It was good to have the knowledge of it – to know what did occur. We were told that Craig had been shot while driving his Warrior in Basra; it was a bit of a freak shot because the bullet got through a tiny gap near his head. We knew that it had been instant.'

In those first few blurred weeks Donna didn't have much time to mourn, busy sorting out her army house; stopping the bills, arranging to move out of it without physically wanting to return to it, and organising the funeral, all as if on autopilot. She didn't have much time to think about Craig. 2 R Welsh was very supportive, saying she could have as long as she wanted to return to the house to clear it. There is no limit on the amount of time a bereaved family can stay in their army quarter and it very much depends on the individual how long they decide to stay. Donna, though, didn't want to return, and the welfare office arranged for some of the other wives to go in and clear the house instead.

The two women worked in silence, picking up every glass or bowl, photo frame or knick-knack and wrapping it carefully in paper as if it was the most precious object in the world. It was just an ordinary army quarter, but the young couple had done their best to make it more than just a house – the photos, cards, the cheerful clutter of their toddler son had made it into a home. After that terrible night when the knock every wife dreads came to her door, Donna never returned from Wales. The moment she had been told he was dead it was no longer their home, just a place they had lived together. The good memories were now eclipsed by the memory of that one horrific night but the house was still filled with their personal belongings. Donna couldn't face the thought of packing their life away, so Amanda – whose husband was regimental sergeant major at the time – and Simone, Amanda's best friend, offered to help. A soldier from the welfare team was sent to help with the heavy lifting but really it was the two women, the two friends, who carried out the sad task.

'I remember looking around and thinking that their whole life together was wrapped up in these walls,' Amanda says. 'It was all so normal – pictures on the walls and cards, all the everyday things that a normal family has, just to make a home and for such a young couple they had made it really lovely.'

Amanda had packed up her home so often during her life as an army wife that picking up the newspaper and folding it expertly around the most awkward of items was second nature to her. But she took more care this day than she ever had before, determined that nothing would get broken and all of Donna's precious possessions would reach her intact. Though Amanda and Simone didn't know Donna they did everything with love and care. It took them a day, and they both found it desperately sad.

The hardest part was the bedroom. The covers were still flung back where Donna had left them and, on the bedside table, was a card with the message on the cover, 'To my loving wife'; neither woman read the inside before placing it in a box. In the wardrobe hung Donna's wedding dress, protected by a plastic covering; next to it was a suit which Simone recognised as Craig's wedding suit from the photograph in pride of place in the couple's living room. There was a photo of Craig and Bradley cuddled up together watching TV, Craig with a bottle of beer and Bradley a bottle of milk – the frame read 'me and my Daddy'.

'It's one of the hardest things I've ever done,' Simone says, 'to go in to somebody's house when he's just died, and see his wedding pictures, wedding suit and shoes – all his personal possessions. You think, "My God, this person has just lost his life." It was absolutely heart-wrenching – to see the photos of his little boy. But we did it because it needed to be done – they wanted two people who were responsible to go in and pack her house up for her, love her, so that's what we did.'

CHAPTER 8

'I Wouldn't Have Known Where To Start, To Rebuild Everything'

Sian was doing the ironing, standing in the hallway of her mum and dad's home. She had wanted to press a top to wear for an afternoon out shopping with her boyfriend, and thought she may as well get a few other bits and pieces sorted while she had the ironing board out. Mum Dereynn was behaving really strangely, rushing around the house, going outside frequently and taking phone calls privately, away from Sian's earshot. She was behaving so out of character that Sian became convinced something was going on. 'Mum kept asking, "Sian, where are you going to be today? Who are you going to be with?" remembers Sian. 'She never usually asks those questions and I asked her if everything was all right. She said that everything was fine, but she just needed to know where I was going to be, and who with, and what time I was going out. I said, "I'm not going out for a while yet," and carried on ironing, but I thought there was something not right – and then she went out, properly this time.'

It was her dad Taff who told Sian what was going on. Arriving home not long after Dereynn had gone out, he explained to his daughter that someone from the battalion had been killed; he didn't say who it was because it was not meant to be made public until the following day. 'Automatically I got this panicked feeling,' says Sian. 'I knew it was someone I knew, because of my mum's reaction throughout the day, and I automatically thought it was Chris – I don't know why.'

Sian stood frozen, with the iron in her hand shaking, then realising she was going to burn herself or her clothes she gently put the iron down on the board, switched it off and tried to breathe. She stood in the hallway, just breathing and thinking, 'This is it, I know it's him.'

Sian and Chris, both twenty-two, had been friends for most of their lives – Chris's dad was also a 2 Royal Welsh soldier and had served alongside Taff, the two children meeting at the age of five when their families were posted to Hong Kong. After Chris's dad left the army, Chris had followed in his father's footsteps, signing up to his dad's battalion and instantly becoming one of the best known, and liked, junior members of the 2 R Welsh. Senior officers and sergeants who had served alongside his father could tell he was a chip off the old block and the younger men warmed to his easy manner and calm professionalism. He was undoubtedly one of Sian's closest friends and she was also mates with his young wife, who now lived near Sian's parents on the patch.

It was not long after Dereynn had fled the house that she called, asking Sian and Taff to come up the road to Dereynn's best friend, fellow Daffodil Girl, Julie's house. Sian left immediately, not stopping to even put shoes on. 'I was power-walking,' she remembers, 'but I thought, "I can't run, because I don't want to get there." Because I just knew. I didn't want to go but I knew I had to be there. My dad came with me, and he was saying, "Sian, calm down," but I said, "No, I know it's him," and he asked, "But who, Sian?" and I said, "I can't talk to you."

At Julie's house Sian could tell that her mum and Julie had been crying. 'It's him isn't it?' Sian asked. 'Who?' asked Dereynn, and Sian responded, 'It's him – don't make me say his name – just tell me yes or no.'

'She didn't even nod, but just looked at me – a little head movement,' Sian says. 'I remember being given a cup of tea but I just blacked out and went into a mess. I remember my mum saying, "'You've still got to go out," and I asked her, "How can you say that to me?" and she said, "I still want you to go out shopping and get away from here." I didn't know how she could say that when half of my existence was being ripped from me and she was telling me to go shopping and forget about it. I know now why she did that, that she was trying to help.'

By this time, Sian's then-boyfriend, Alex, was waiting for her to meet him, so Dereynn left Sian with Julie and went to tell him what was going on. Alex was due to go to Afghanistan a few months later but Sian couldn't even think about that. 'All I could think about was Chris's wife, Danielle, and his mum and dad, and brother,' remembers Sian. 'It was like a loop tape, over and over in my mind but

I still didn't think it was real, not really. It was only a few days later when he was named in the press that I could believe it.'

It was a sunny August day and Mandy was watching her son training with the under-tens rugby team in Andover when her phone rang. It was one of the wives ringing in a state because it was being reported on the lunchtime news that someone had been killed in Afghanistan – at this point no details had been released. This phone call was the first of many, as all the wives from A company – serving in Helmand – started to panic. Mandy, more experienced than most and with a husband playing a senior role out there as Company sergeant major, tried to reassure them. She had complete faith in the families' office and had been trying to get the wives to understand from day one that if it was your husband, then someone would knock on your door to inform you – you're not going to hear from the media, or by telephone, or your best mate, or neighbour. 'We're protected in that sense,' Mandy explains. 'If there is, God forbid, a death, or a casualty, it isn't going to come by word of mouth. The information will come to you from those it's meant to come from. I had great faith in that.'

Half an hour after her phone first rang Mandy received a call from Mo, telling her that it was indeed one of the 2 R Welsh lads. 'I didn't know the soldier personally,' says Mandy, 'but the emotion was quite overwhelming – it made the surreal real. It brought it home to me what danger not only my husband but all of them, were in.'

Because Mo had called Mandy, she knew one hundred per cent that husband Ian was OK – even though she had known logically it wasn't him, and reassured the other wives that the system was infallible, Mandy couldn't help but feel a huge wave of relief. 'That, I suppose, is the selfish thing when you've got loved ones out there,' she explains, 'because you do initially give your loved one a thought, as well as feeling the emotion for the person who has lost their life. You feel guilt for the relief – because although your husband might be OK somewhere else people have lost a son, husband, dad and they are connected to you through the battalion. Then you feel terribly sad to imagine what hurt that family must be feeling at that time, knowing the person they love is dead. I can't begin to imagine what that must feel like – I will never forget the faces of the two mothers of the boys that lost their lives that tour. Talking about it, it still feels as raw as the day I heard it. It's one of those things of war, as politicians would say, but as a mother of a boy as well, I can't bear to think of it.'

Chris's father was in the regiment at the same time as Dai – so Julie had known the family for years; her eldest son used to go to karate with Chris and Julie, like the rest of the battalion had watched him grow from confident child to brave infantryman. As Julie puts it, 'He was like the son of the regiment. When someone is lost it is terrible, but Chris affected everybody because we'd seen him grow up. It was a big, big shock. I think of Chris, a young boy like that, and you just think, "Why Chris?" The same with Craig – why Craig? Why any of them? As a regiment we've had a lot of losses, it doesn't get any easier, but you've got to carry on with your life, because if you don't . . . I've got to think that I've got two children to look after and you can't be in pieces when you've got children. When my boys go to bed that's when I'll have my little cry, but I don't do it in front of them. I'll be brave for them.'

One of the strangest feelings for the Daffodil Girls is when this private moment of grief becomes public property: suddenly, their story is in the full glare of the media. When Craig was killed in Iraq, Julie knew that someone from the battalion had been killed but she couldn't put a face to the name. Much junior in age and rank to her husband, Craig was not someone she had spent time with but when, a few days after he was killed, she opened her newspaper to see his picture, lying across his Warrior tank smiling out from the newspaper page at her she broke down in tears. 'I knew that we had lost somebody – I knew the name but I couldn't put a picture to him,' she says. 'When Craig was in the paper I just cried, because I realised I had spoken with him just before he left – me and Dereynn – we were having a laugh with him, a bit of banter. He was talking about his wife, about how she does all the cooking and I said, "We'll have to introduce ourselves while you're away – me and Dereynn – and tell her how you've got to do your share in the house." We had a laugh with him – and that was the last time we saw him.'

Working in camp for a cleaning firm, Dereynn got to know more of the younger lads, junior in rank to her husband, than some of the other wives did. So when she opened her copy of *The Sun* she recognised the face smiling up at her instantly; Craig, whom, despite his height, she and

Julie had nicknamed 'the cheeky little man'. 'He used to make us laugh,' she recalls. 'We'd be cleaning the guardroom, and he'd be telling us that he was getting married and how "she'd be under the thumb" and we'd say to him, "Stop it now. Once the wife comes down make sure you get her to coffee mornings and she gets out and meets people." Then you hear that news that somebody's been killed, and you think, "Right . . ." and you think, "Craig – and the name doesn't ring a bell," but you know he's of the battalion. I got the newspaper and opened it up, and my choice of language was not nice. I just thought it was not fair. There he was, the cheeky little man, sitting on the tank and you know that's one that's gone.

'You get to know the younger boys and you do feel like a mother to them. I think, "I've got kids your age." When Chris died it was terrible – I met him first in Hong Kong and he lived in the same block as we did. He must have been about five. You ask yourself why him – it's nasty, he had more to give – but You had to take him away. I take my hat off to his wife and I admire the strength she has, because I wouldn't have known where to start, to rebuild everything. You've just lost a partner, a friend – a soul-mate – how do you carry on after that? You sit there and wonder why, you think, "Is there a God out there – because if there is one, why are they doing this, taking people away? Why do this to families and leaving them in so much grief?" A very brave lady, his wife is – and his mum and dad, and I look at them and think it's not fair.

'Nothing's fair in this day and age, but we're still there and fighting – and smiling, even though it's been a hard day.

You'd be having a hard day and Chris would pop into your head, or "cheeky little man" pops into your head. You can't be having a bad day then, can you? Your day is bound to be going to be better than that of those families – I don't know where they start. Each and every one of them who have lost someone, there's a mum and dad who have lost a son and a wife who's lost her husband – a child that's lost their dad, grandparents who have lost a grandchild. It's hard to think that they have to live their lives now with just pictures of the person they love.'

When she heard that Chris had been killed, all that Kaz wanted was to speak to her husband. Even though she hadn't known Chris, he was in the same company as Brian and Kaz knew that her husband would have known him and, in all likelihood, been nearby when he was killed. Kaz wanted to support her husband but was also desperate to hear his voice, the terrible news of Chris's death serving as a reminder – if one was needed – of quite how dangerous it was where they were stationed. Brian didn't call for the first couple of days after Chris's death – 'OP MINIMISE was active – and when he was finally able to use the phone, Kaz was out at a friend's. Brian had tried the landline of their house and was annoyed when he couldn't reach his wife. He tried the mobile and, upset, berated his wife for not being there for him when he called, saying, 'You're never there.' Kaz recalls, 'I went inside and said to my friend Emma that he was really off with me. I was quite upset – I thought, "What do you want me to do, Bri? I can't sit inside alone all the time you're away," Then the phone went again, and he'd rung back, and he said, "I'm really sorry, I shouldn't have taken it out on you."'

Brian explained that he had been there when Chris was killed and had just been interviewed by a senior officer, as they tried to piece together what had happened. The men had been on patrol and Chris had been killed when he stepped on an IED (improvised explosive device). Brian was only metres away and was deeply shocked by the death of his colleague. After the explosion the men went into three hours of intense combat – no time to grieve when you are in a war zone. Brian told his wife that before they left camp, for what would be Chris's last patrol, he had seen Chris take out the photo of Danielle that he always carried in his top pocket and kiss it tenderly before carefully placing it back. It was something that Brian would never forget and the story brought hot tears to Kaz's eyes – even though she didn't know the couple.

It is ironic that the time when you most need to speak to the person you love is the time when you can't. When the news would come in of a death in Iraq while Ed was there (and twenty-three military personnel lost their lives during this time, making it one of the deadliest periods of modern conflict for the British Army) all I would want to do is speak to him, to reassure myself by hearing his voice and offer him any support he needed. Other than the women in the same position as me, he was the only person who I knew would understand how I was feeling, the mixed feelings of sadness and relief, guilt and the fear that the next time we might not be so lucky. But of course OP MINIMISE would be in place until the family had been informed and given some time to inform their nearest and dearest before the media was allowed to release a name. It wouldn't take that long – normally within twenty-four hours of the MOD announcing that 'A soldier has been killed in an incident in Basra, the next of kin have requested a period of grace before further details are released.' You would wait for your phone to ring, aware that even when the phones were opened, the queues at this window of opportunity would be great and, during the time Ed was in Iraq with heavy losses and casualties par for the course, OP MINIMISE could be back on before he had a chance to get to the phone. Ed would do his best – calling even if it was just for a minute to reassure me he was 'fine, miles from the incident, perfectly safe, honest'. So a death that causes total devastation for one family has a ripple effect, filtering all the way down to those couples who have no connection to the deceased, but mourn nonetheless and are forced to face the brutal reality of their present situation, the danger and the separation they are enduring.

Julie was the regimental sergeant major's wife so, together with the commanding officer's wife and Dereynn, she went to see Danielle a couple of days after Chris had been killed. She didn't know Danielle but whenever she had seen Chris and his young wife out and about, even from a distance, Chris would greet Julie with a cheery bellow of 'Hiya', so Danielle knew who she was. 'As soon as I looked at her,' Julie remembers, 'I wondered what I was going to say to her. I didn't know – I looked at her and she just shrugged her shoulders. I said, "I don't know what to say." I just gave her a big massive hug. She is such a brave girl, she is. I remember when I hugged her, the shaking on her. I'll never forget that. I wanted to help her but there was nothing I could do. Hard.'

It was a few days after the news that her childhood friend had been killed when Sian's mum suggested they do something, something symbolic to show they were thinking about Chris, his wife and family. Dereynn suggested that they buy some flowers and go and lay them in camp by the main clock – it was a small gesture but one that she hoped might help Sian to start to accept that Chris was gone. They walked the short distance from Dereynn's house on the Matthews estate to the supermarket to buy a bunch but once inside Sian found she could only stand and stare at the colourful array of plants and flowers displayed close to the entrance. 'I remember thinking "What am I doing?" then I got really angry,' says Sian. 'My mum said, "What flowers do you want?" and I said, "Who the fuck cares – they're going to die and there's no point in buying them. What's the point?" Chris was dead and I was having an argument in a shop with my mother about flowers.'

Then Sian heard her name being called, she turned to see Rachel, the older sister of Chris's widow, and a friend and neighbour of Sian's, standing with Rachel's mum. The two girls went to one another and hugged, not sure whom was comforting whom. When Rachel pulled away, Sian realised that Danielle, Chris's wife, was standing behind them. Sian felt herself crumple and not knowing what to say murmured, 'How are you?' Afterwards, she would ask herself why she asked such a stupid question when she knew the only answer could be – 'Devastated'. Danielle didn't answer at first, she just stood looking dazed and pale but at the same time composed, 'I can't believe this, Sian,' she finally said and Sian could see the pain etched on her pretty features. Sian replied, 'No, no one can. I can't get my head around it.' The girls hugged, Sian squeezing her friend tightly while she mumbled support in her ear, 'We all love you, we are all here for you, we all cared about Chris.' When they finally pulled apart, Danielle's mum and sister led her outside; they weren't actually shopping and had only left the house to get some fresh air, to try and get Danielle out. Sian watched them walk away. 'Danielle looked very small, like a little girl lost – that's when the penny dropped with me, there in Tesco,' remembers Sian. 'I completely broke down as I realised the next time I saw Chris it would be when he was being carried in to church. I turned back to the flowers and chose some – I bought him yellow roses.'

Sian decided not to attend the memorial in camp; like Amanda she was working at Help for Heroes and they both decided that they would each take one day off – Amanda would go to the memorial in Tidworth, Sian to the funeral in Wales.

Dereynn and Taff went with Amanda to the memorial and when they came home, ashen-faced and weary with emotion, they told Sian how it had been. 'Mum said, "They brought him in," Sian recalls. 'I asked what she meant, and she said, "They've brought him on to camp, Sian." I was glad I hadn't seen that.' Sian hadn't seen Danielle since they met in Tesco and decided that she needed to see her, and the rest of Chris's family, before the funeral. She knew that if the first time she saw them was at the funeral she wouldn't know what to say. So, a few days later, Dereynn and Sian went to Danielle's mum's house to see them; Danielle was staying there with Chris's parents and younger brother. They all sat in the living room and talked about Chris – Dereynn and Julie had known Chris's parents for years and had watched Chris grow up and were as devastated by his death as Sian was. 'There wasn't anything profound said that day,' Sian remembers, 'but we just reminisced about the good times – someone would tell a story, remember something funny Chris had said or done. You'd laugh so hard at the memory – then five minutes later there would be a dead silence, because of the realisation that there would be no new stories about Chris, that he wouldn't make us laugh ever again.'

Kaz had found out about Chris through a friend, as the terrible news started to spread through the wives' network. Danielle had rung a couple of her close friends so it had got out in the area and some of the wives knew who it was before he was named in the news. Kaz hadn't known Chris but, she explains, even if you don't know the 2 R Welsh soldier killed, they're still part of the family. 'For some wife that you don't know to lose their husband is almost like you losing a member of your family because it is such a close company. You really just don't know what to do to make things any better for them.' The first time Kaz saw Danielle was when they went to the service on the square for Chris and she really didn't know what to say but she found she was able to speak to Chris's mother, murmuring how sorry she was, what a fine young soldier he had been. Kaz didn't know Chris's mum before but she was a former Daffodil

Girl, so the two women had things in common. 'She's now a friend on Facebook,' Kaz says, 'so we've got friendly since this has happened. The strength of that woman is unbelievable – I really admire her. Danielle is absolutely fantastic. They are amazing people.'

Elaine agrees. 'I didn't know Danielle to talk to – just to say hello – but I met her properly at the memorial,' she explains. 'She was lovely – and she was strong, but you could feel her heartbreak – it was devastating. Chris's family and Danielle were crying, surrounded by women whose husbands were still over there and I knew they were thinking the same way as me, that it could have been me, and it still could be.'

Elaine was wearing black; she'd come from work and decided not to change, feeling the colour was appropriate. It was a sunny March day and they stood on the parade ground. Chris's coffin was brought on and the padre said a few prayers, hymns were sung before the coffin was taken away again and then everyone went to the warrant officers' and sergeants' mess to have a cup of tea. The family and Danielle were there. 'I went and spoke to her,' Elaine remembers. I said, "I'm sorry." And I spoke to Chris's mum, and she said something about Pete still being over there. I said, "Yeah . . ." and she said I was brave. She was lovely.'

Elaine hadn't known Chris or Danielle well, but with her husband still out in Afghanistan, she shared the instincts of so many of the Daffodil Girls, of wanting to pay her respects. It's not an easy thing to go through when your husband remains out on the front line. Chris was killed during the first month of the tour, and Elaine's husband Pete still had five long months to go. As she watched Danielle, bravely holding it together, all Elaine could think was 'It could have been me – and it could still be me.'

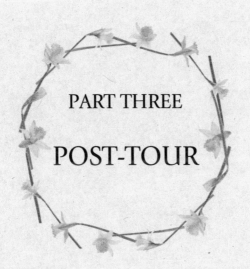

PART THREE

POST-TOUR

CHAPTER 1

'That Was The Hardest Bit, Watching Him Being Carried In'

Amanda was freezing, standing on the parade ground. It was December and late afternoon, dark and bitterly cold. Despite being wrapped up in hat, scarf, gloves and thick winter coat, she still needed to blow on her fingers and stamp her feet to keep the feeling in them. She was flanked by her two daughters, the girls every so often putting their arms around their mum and giving her a squeeze to help them all warm up. Around them stood the other Daffodil Girls; wives, mothers and daughters of the 2nd Royal Welsh, small children clutching flags. The atmosphere was one of huge excitement: the long six months were finally over – the boys were coming home.

Then, from around the corner they heard the distinct rumble of a Warrior tank starting up before the band of The Royal Welsh started to play. As regimental sergeant major, it was Lee's job to march the men on to the parade ground and eventually release them, into the arms of their waiting families. 'I could hear Lee long before I could see him; I remember feeling really proud and then there they were, the men marching to stand in front of us, Lee leading the way.'

The couple half-walked, half-ran to one another and embraced, their daughters piling in so the family were reunited in one big *cwtch* (welsh for hug). 'Lee's eyes were watering,' Amanda remembers, 'but he said it was because of the wind. Mine and the girls were watering too, but we were happy to admit we were welling up because we were so pleased to see him; it was very emotional.'

Any of the Daffodil Girls will tell you that one of the best things about being an army wife are the homecomings. I have irritated many a 'civvy' couple by telling them that they may not go through the lows experienced by army couples, but they will also certainly be unlikely to experience quite the same highs either. When Ed came back from Iraq, I was more excited than I think I have ever been before in my life – it was better than all the Christmases or birthdays I had ever known, and I would even go as far as to say it was as happy and exciting a day as our wedding day would be a few years later.

Ed came home earlier than the rest of the regiment, just by a week, as he had to work on a handover for his next job. So ours was a private reunion, once again back at Brize Norton, but the feeling was completely different from R&R. Because alongside the excitement of seeing him again was the biggest sense of relief I have ever experienced. I did not realise quite how stressed and anxious I had been until he walked through those revolving doors, tour over, and I could feel the weight literally lifting from my shoulders.

Ed has been away a few times since that tour – for months at a time training, where contact is as limited as it is when the men are on the front line. But I haven't worried about him; it was just his absence that was the problem, and these homecomings are also magical. Amanda sums it up, 'If they are away – be it on tour or a period away from home training, the homecoming is always amazing. They say that absence makes the heart grow fonder – and it does.' Simone agrees, 'In the relationship, the homecomings are the highs. Over the years, going back to when I was younger, I'd hear older wives saying, "Can't wait for him to go away again."'

'I wondered if I'd ever find myself saying that but I never have. If he goes away for four or five days, here or there, that's nothing, it's even quite nice, but I've never wished him to go away on tour or for longer than a few days. That feeling when they come home takes you back to when you were a teenager, you've got the butterflies in the stomach; it's like when you were first dating. We've been married for nineteen years, and yet I still want to make sure my hair and make-up are perfect and I've wearing a nice, normally new, outfit before he walks through that door, or I go to meet him. I'm glad I feel like that because if I didn't I'd be worried.'

Like Ed, Taff came back earlier than the other men on the battalion's tour of Iraq. Dereynn hadn't told the children. Even though their two are both adults now, Dereynn doesn't like telling them exactly when their father is coming back.

She wants it to be a surprise, yet still let them get excited – so she tends to tell them that it will be a few days' later than he is really due back; also hoping that, as they aren't expecting him, if he is delayed it will spare them any disappointment. This most recent homecoming, she told their children he would be back on the Thursday when really it was two days earlier. Gav, their son, was at college and Sian at university, so Dereynn decorated the outside of their army quarter with a 'Welcome Home Dad' banner and balloons, with the help of Julie and a few other friends. The other families in the small cul-de-sac where they lived were all smiles to see the banners up, knowing what a long six months it had been for their neighbour. When Gav came home he saw the decorations and asked Dereynn when Taff was due and Dereynn couldn't repress the grin as she gave the answer that made her son's face split in a wide smile – 'Dad's on his way.'

Dereynn could barely contain her excitement as she waited for the car bringing her husband home, then the car pulled up and Julie and Dereynn's other friends started clapping. 'I was thinking, "Oh my God, he's home,"' Dereynn recalls. 'I'm like a little kid again, like when we first met, wondering, "What do I do now?" It's nerve-racking – and that's after twenty-odd years of marriage. He came up to me and I gave him a kiss and a *cwtch* – and he's home.

'Your body seems to relax – something seems to lift from you, you know for the first time in months you're going to go to bed and you're going to sleep properly because he's there.' The couple went into their house and shared a kiss in the hallway and then, recalls Dereynn with a laugh, 'He starts following me around. His great thing is that he likes to have a bath when he comes in – it's all showers out there. I ask him if he'd like a cup of coffee – then once I've done that, that's it, I've done you the first one, and now you can do the rest. You're home now. That's it. I'm off all the duties and it's your turn now.'

Despite an equally long marriage, Julie also didn't know quite what to do when husband Dai came home from his last tour. Like Taff he did not come back with the bulk of the battalion; he was collected by a minibus with a couple of others and dropped at the parade ground in camp. It was a bit nippy that day so Julie decided to wear jeans and a jumper; she had a shower and got ready, not bothering with make-up as she prefers to be natural unless she's going on a night out. She said to her boys, 'Come on, let's go and see your dad,' and they piled into her car in high excitement. Clutching the flags Julie had got them to wave, they drove into camp, collecting mate Dereynn, who was coming to keep Julie company in case the minibus was delayed.

Not long after arriving in camp the minibus rounded the corner and Dai jumped out. 'I just looked at him, I didn't know what to do,' Julie tells me. 'I felt like a little schoolgirl, nervous, excited, shy all at the same time I didn't know whether to run and hug him or wait for him to come to me; I was frozen, as were the boys.' At that point Dereynn broke the ice by going forward to envelope Dai in a bear-hug, breaking Julie out of her trance and prompting her to run forward to her husband. 'Then as soon as I gave Dai a *cwtch*, the kids ran up and *cwtched* him too.' She recalls, 'I don't think they knew what to do either. It was like I was going out on a date with this stranger. I know they come home on R&R, but after that it's another three months till you see them again and you know that this time they come home and they're going to be staying with you and you will have to readjust to one another, and as a family.'

It was a beautiful summer's day when it was time for Brian to come home to Kaz. Kaz and the fellow C Company wives had been told to be in camp by 2 pm ready to greet their husbands. Kaz had gained a little bit of weight while Brian had been away and was worried that he would notice, but thankfully her excitement overrode her nerves and she felt pretty in her new orange dress, which she was wearing with brown leggings and a little olive scarf tied loosely round her neck. Once in camp most of the ladies helped themselves to a glass of wine from the Prince of Wales bar to try and calm their excitement; they still had an hour to go as the men weren't due back until 3 pm. Three o'clock came and went, then four, then five, by which point the Prince of Wales was filled with slightly merry wives and terribly overexcited children. They were playing together but occasionally running back to grab mum and ask, 'How long till Daddy gets here?' to which the only response could be 'soon'.

Finally, at ten to six, the families were asked to gather on the parade square and the men marched on. 'It was such an overwhelming feeling,' Kaz says, 'and I couldn't find him – all the wives and children were clapping, then running to their soldier and I couldn't see Bri in the crowd. My daughter spotted him before I did, so she was the first one to grab hold of him and have a *cwtch*. But I'll never forget his first words when he saw me – he just said "Wow." I thought it was so sweet – I'd put on weight, but he was still . . . you know. I think he was just ready to be home, really. He was wearing his deserts and had lost lots of weight – all of the men looked absolutely shattered. I couldn't believe he was here and wasn't going back. It was lovely.'

Not every homecoming is as joyous an occasion as it was for Kaz and Brian. There is a second kind of homecoming, and this second kind is, sadly, a sombre and poignant occasion. It had been another summer's day when Craig was flown home, but unlike the warm sunshine of Brian's return, this was a chilly August day, a thick layer of cloud blocking out any summer sun that might have been trying to make an appearance.

It was over a week after Craig had been killed: three other young men had died around the same time as him, so there had been a wait to organise all four being flown home together. It was, in Donna's words, a horrific day. The evening before they had travelled up as a family – Donna, Craig's mum and grandparents – in a bus provided by the army, and stayed in a hotel for the night so they could be at RAF Lyneham the next morning. Donna had left her son Bradley with a friend, feeling he was too young to be attend. They gathered just before eleven at the military airport, but because of the weather they were not able to watch the plane perform its fly-past outside, near the tarmac runway. Instead, they were ushered to a room where, alongside the families of the three other men being brought home, they could watch the plane come into land on a large television screen.

Donna was wearing black, as were most of the other people in the room, with the men in suits and ties. One by one the coffins were borne off the C-17 transport aircraft. Each was draped in the Union Flag and carried by six men dressed in their service dress uniform. Craig's coffin was the fourth off. For Donna, almost the worst part was watching the agony of the other families as their loved ones were carried off the plane and on to the tarmac, until it was Craig's turn. 'It was nice to know he was back in the country – home with us,' Donna remembers. 'He was carried out by his mates, which I was pleased about and he would have liked, but it was still awful.'

Craig's coffin was placed in the hearse and taken to Oxford for the post-mortem, before being released back to the family in Wales. Then, at the local undertakers, Donna was able to visit her husband for the first time. It felt like only yesterday that they had kissed goodbye – Craig lifting Donna down from the kitchen chair and promising that he would see her soon – and she knew that it wasn't until she could actually see him, in the coffin, that she would be able to believe he was really dead and wouldn't be keeping his promise to come home safely. They were, in Donna's words, 'lucky' to be able to have an open coffin so, she explains, they could see and touch him. 'That was lovely, because some of the families aren't so lucky,' she says. 'He was all in one piece and they could hide where the bullet had gone in.'

This was Donna's first experience of death so although she wanted to see Craig, and wanted confirmation that the anonymous coffin really did contain her husband, the twenty-one-year-old widow was also scared. Craig's mother went in first – as a nurse she felt able to see her son and check that it would be OK for Donna and Craig's little sister to come in too. Donna entered the room slowly, clutching the hand of her visiting officer from 2 R Welsh. 'I didn't really know what to expect,' she remembers. 'It was lovely that I could see him, but I was howling. Even then, it still didn't click fully in my head that it was true, even though I was stood there. I expecting him to be taking the mick, because that's the sort of person he was. I kept expected him to jump up and laugh at us for believing he was really dead. He was wearing the clothes I'd gone on a shopping trip to buy him. It was nice that I could do that, but it was awful buying just one pair of boxers, one pair of socks, instead of a pack which I would normally buy, because there was no point buying more than one – he would never need them after that.'

Donna knew that the first thing Craig would have done when he came home from Iraq was to go out and buy the new Wales rugby kit, the updated version of the one he had been wearing when they had met just three years before. So she bought that and some comfortable tracksuit bottoms. 'We did think about putting him in his army uniform,' she recalls, 'but although that was the job he was in and he loved it, as soon as he got home, his kit would be off and he would wear something more comfortable. So I wanted him to be wearing something he would have worn at home, after work, just hanging out with me and Bradley. It was a surreal shopping trip but I enjoyed it because it was one of the last things I could do for him – apart from the funeral.'

It was a crisp, clear October day when James returned to the UK. The previous evening his mother Sarah, his sister

Emma and brother Josh, Emma's boyfriend Tom as well as James's father Nigel, had all come up from Wales on transport provided by the army and had also spent the night in a hotel near RAF Lyneham. They needed to be at the military airport first thing because at 11 am the huge C-17 aircraft bringing home James's body would do a slow fly-past before landing on the airfield tarmac. Limited numbers of people were able to be at the airport, so sixty or so of James's wider family and many friends had also arrived to be at Wootton Bassett where, alongside hundreds of locals, they would be able to pay their respects as the hearse bearing James's body travelled from RAF Lyneham to a hospital in Oxford where the post-mortem would be carried out.

Sarah stood to the side of the airfield under a canopy, flanked by her two children, the family watching in silence as the large grey, windowless plane flew by, the pilot dipping the wing towards them as he passed as a mark of respect. It circled, then landed. Seven men marched forward, sombre and smart in their khaki service dress uniform. Six of the men, the ones who would carry the coffin from the plane to the waiting hearse, were James's peers – junior soldiers from the battalion. The last soldier was a sergeant major, there to lead the men.

The back of the aeroplane opened, a ramp lowered to give access to the yawning cavern inside. The men marched forward together, in height order – the shortest at the front with the taller bringing up the rear. They disappeared into the aircraft. A bugler then began to play the haunting first notes of *The Last Post* and the men started to exit the C-17 carrying James. His coffin wrapped in the Union Flag, they walked to the waiting hearse, a modern Mercedes with glass sides and roof to enable a clear view of the coffin, and loaded their brother soldier into it with the utmost care and respect. Then, the hearse was driven off the tarmac while the men stood to attention and the bugler played *Reveille*.

'Everybody was so gentle and lovely with us there,' Sarah remembers, 'but the reality of seeing that plane, that huge plane with just James coming off on his own – it was haunting. We were told that we had to stand underneath a canopy because there were cameras above us and they're not allowed to film the families, but as soon as I could see him all I wanted to do was run to him. We weren't able to see him at this point, but before they took him to Oxford we were able to go into the chapel of rest where they put him in his open coffin. I went to see him and he just looked perfect. I just wanted to wrap my arms round him.'

Sarah didn't want James to have a military funeral at first; she wanted him buried as James her son, not a soldier. But when she read the tributes posted on the MOD website by the soldiers who had served alongside him and by the company commander, Rhiannon's husband Huw, she changed her mind. 'That was his life, and he was happy with what he was doing,' she explains. 'There were a few videos put on Facebook of him in various situations in the army and in every one he was smiling. There were photos too, from his time in Afghanistan and in every one he's just stood there with a smile on his face, so we thought he deserved to have the military funeral and we went with that.'

Rhiannon was at James's funeral. As the wife of Huw, James's company commander, she felt it was only right that she should attend as, still out in Afghanistan, Huw was unable to do so. She travelled down to Wales with the second in command of the battalion, Matt, and his wife. When they arrived they were far too early so they decided to get a coffee before the ceremony began. 'We couldn't find anywhere,' Rhiannon remembers, 'and we asked an old lady at a bus stop and she directed us to this builders' cafe. We decided to order some food and had these massive doorstep bacon sandwiches – ridiculous size. It was eight o'clock in the morning and we were all obviously dressed for a funeral – so everyone in that town knew why we were there, and that we were military and they couldn't do enough for us – even in this little builders' cafe. We walked up the hill to the church and there were crowds of people with banners and flags. People wanted to be there – and they'd waited outside for two hours just to support the family, even though there would be no room in the church and even though they didn't know James, it was lovely.'

The streets of James's home town of Cwmbran were lined with people. Sarah remembers firemen, allowed out of work to show their respect, and groups of schoolchildren. The church was at the top of a steep hill, so the hearse stopped and James's Union Flag-draped coffin was carried into the church along with white and red floral tributes spelling the words 'Welsh warrior' and depicting the Prince of Wales's Feathers. 'That was the hardest bit,' says Sarah, 'watching him being carried in.'

Rhiannon remembers watching the flag-draped coffin arrive in the church. 'This was the second time I'd seen it done like that, the first was at the funeral of the lad killed just before James. I didn't even realise we did that – I'd only seen it in American films. Seeing the coffin covered in the Union Jack just made me cry; it's so emotive – it just brings it home to you, it's horrible. The bearers weren't military; instead they were six of his friends and family, young people.'

Following the first hymn, fourteen of James's closest friends gathered in front of the altar and each read a line of a poem they had written in tribute to him. The poem included the lines, 'Some people will say "another fallen soldier", we don't agree, you're a great Welsh warrior.' 'It was beautiful,' says Rhiannon, 'you can't say anything else about it. They were so brave, and some of the girls were barely getting through it, but they held one another up and they finished together.' The padre then read out excerpts from a school essay James's younger brother Josh had written, just days before his death, about how proud he was of his sibling. 'It took one year for my brother to become a soldier, fighting for us and his country,' Josh had written. 'I'm very proud of him and what he has become in just one year.'

'That was lovely,' remembers Sarah, 'the poem and what Josh had written. Then we listened to stories about him in the army, and how they talked about him, how much he was liked and respected. People say, "You must be so proud of him," but I was proud of him before he went in the army, and I was proud of him as a boy – as the young man he grew into. He was just a good kid and it shone out, and that day it shone out. But still none of it seemed real and, it still doesn't – and I wish it wasn't.'

*

Hundreds of people had turned out to line the streets along the two-and-a-half mile route through Craig's home village, Blaengarw. Welsh flags hung from windows or billowed on flagpoles in gardens, and many shops and small businesses were closed as a mark of respect. A glass carriage, drawn by two black horses, carried the coffin, which was draped in the Union Flag and topped with a flower arrangement that read simply 'Daddy'. It started at the top of the Carn, which was the highest point of the valley, outside Craig's beloved nan's house. Nanny Carn (as the children had always called her) had cancer and was too frail to attend the funeral; this way she could watch from the window as the carriage carrying her grandson started on its sad, slow, descent down the hill. Donna, along with Craig's immediate family, walked behind the carriage to begin with then, at the bottom of the hill, they got into some waiting funeral cars.

It was a clear and warm day but Donna still had goosebumps on her arms. She looked out of the window to see the streets lined with strangers, Welsh flags in hand, heads bowed as the funeral procession passed, there to honour her husband. 'It was something I'd never seen in my life before,' she remembers. 'Everybody closed their shops and the whole valley must have been out – it was unbelievable. It was so emotional, but I was full of pride. All my family had come down, and my dad, who's sixty-five now; he said afterwards that he'd never seen anything like it, with people lining the road, and it was something he would take to his grave – the community spirit. Where we're from, we don't have anything like that.'

The procession stopped outside Craig's mother's house

where the soldier had been raised and where his widow and young son were now living. A group of Craig's friends, local boys not soldiers, stood to attention as the carriage came to a halt, saluting their childhood friend. Donna felt the first of the many tears that rolled down her face that day. At the crematorium the gates had to be shut due to media interest, paparazzi trying to get a picture. 'They were standing on the wall trying to get pictures,' recalls Donna, 'it was like being a film star – but in an awful way.'

Craig was carried into the chapel by six 2 R Welsh peers; the service was given a ninety-minute time allocation, far longer than the normal half-hour. Because of the number who wanted to pay tribute to the young soldier, the small room was filled completely, with many people having to stand or wait outside. 'We had so many people talking, from the headmaster from his old school, to his sisters, his best friend who was his neighbour – his friends who had saluted him.' Donna recalls with a half-smile. 'A lot of it is a blur now – I can't remember a lot of what was said, because it was so emotional. It was so lovely though.'

Amanda was one of the guests at Craig's funeral; wife of the current regimental sergeant major, she had wanted to attend on behalf of her husband, still out in Iraq. After clearing out Donna's home following Craig's death, she felt close to the young couple and wanted to pay her own respects. 'I attended all of the funerals on behalf of the wives of the regiment, and the families of 2 Royal Welsh,' she explains. However difficult it was for her, she knew how hard it was for her husband as well. 'That tour he played a role in sixteen or seventeen repatriations, the ceremony held in Iraq when those killed are sent home, for our boys and boys from other regiments. And all of those must still stay with him, just like those funerals do with me.'

Craig was the third young 2 R Welsh soldier to be killed that tour, so his was the third funeral that Amanda had attended. 'I felt anger towards everything,' she remembers, 'why was this happening again? I don't think my anger was directed at anyone or anything in particular – it was more a feeling of, "My God, why is this happening again?" And I was not just angry – I felt slightly hardened to it as well, because I'd attended two funerals in very quick succession, and I felt more composed in myself. I thought my emotions were not as raw as with the first two.'

But when the service began Amanda realised that this was not the case. 'I didn't realise that Craig's family had requested that there be no flowers, and we provided, as we did for all the soldiers killed, the three-feathers floral tribute and the cap badge. So when the coffin was brought down, they were the only flowers on it apart from the "Daddy" tribute that the family had brought. To see those flowers, the cap badge, made it really hard, I don't know why. The service was conducted in Welsh and English – which made it even more moving. I don't understand Welsh, but you understand what's going on behind the words – he was a brave Welsh warrior, so it was appropriate to have it done in both languages. His mother was so articulate when she got up and spoke. His sister got up and said a poem – it was so moving and Craig's turned out to be, for me, the hardest funeral to cope with, emotionally.'

At the end of the service three volleys of gunfire were shot, and Donna remembers jumping in fright, before *The Last Post* was sounded by a bugler. 'That gets me every time now and I can't listen to it,' she says. The family had asked for Craig's coffin not to be moved while they were in the crematorium, not wanting to see it go behind the curtain.

Outside the crematorium the commanding officer of 2 R Welsh presented Donna with the flag from Craig's coffin, folded into a triangle, with his beret and medal placed on top. 'I didn't know what to do and I was crying,' she remembers. 'I turned to ask someone what I should do but it seemed that everybody I knew wasn't there at that moment – it was all strangers. Somebody took it off me, I think – I was in a daze and I didn't know what I was doing. But then I found everybody and had a cigarette to calm my nerves.'

The wake was held in the local rugby club. Donna collected Bradley on the way: she had left him with a friend, feeling that seeing the coffin and coming to the crematorium would be too much for the little boy, but she felt that it was important for him to be part of the party to celebrate his dad's life. In the weeks before Craig's departure for Iraq the young couple had avoided talking too much about the sad 'what ifs' but Donna was glad now to know two things he wanted – where he wanted his ashes to be scattered and which friend he wanted to sing at the wake. At the time, Craig only mentioned a nickname and it was not a friend Donna knew, but after Craig was killed she asked around and managed to track down the friend that Craig wanted to perform.

'Chubby' sang a few of Craig's favourites, including Bob Dylan's *Knockin' on Heaven's Door* and *Teenage Kicks* by the Undertones, which raised smiles from the guests. Once he had finished, Chubby left his microphone, set up with speakers, on stage. Three-year-old Bradley climbed up there and decided to have a go, grabbing hold of the mike and launching into a made-up song which, within seconds; had the whole room laughing. When he had appeared to have finished everyone cheered and clapped and Craig's sister and friend went up to get him down, but apparently the little boy's performance wasn't over. 'He threw a complete paddy,' Donna remembers with a smile, 'and there was shouting and applauding in the audience, booing as they wrestled the mike from him. Everybody loved it – and Craig would have loved it, he'd have said, "That's my boy."'

CHAPTER 2

'He Went Through A Lot
And Saw A Lot Of Terrible Things . . .'

There is a booklet that is given out to soldiers and their wives, post-tour, to offer guidance for the sometimes difficult period of readjustment. It has changed over the years, but the gist is the same.

For the soldier, it says, be realistic: everyone has changed, communications will be difficult at first. Take a while to get to know one another again, interests may have changed, any older problems will still exist. Don't change systems that have been working well in your absence. Don't find fault or criticise, go easy on discipline with the children. Take some time to understand how the family has changed during the separation, spend some time with the entire family before taking time alone with your partner. Expect some sexual tensions, talk to loved ones, listen to your spouse, support positive changes, show an interest in how the family has changed, and expect to make some adjustments.

For the wife, it advises making the homecoming parade special. Stay confident, stay flexible, negotiate activities. Make time for you as a couple. Adjust gradually, start with small changes and make them slowly. Be patient, don't expect everything to happen at once. Re-adjustment takes time.

This is all sensible advice and obvious in many ways. But in reality, how easy is it for a couple to follow these guidelines? Simone readily admits that she was hopeless at adhering to such advice. 'When he [Mark] comes home at the end of a tour, the amazing feelings of butterflies and romance lasts a good few days, but as this is real, unlike R&R which is more like a honeymoon than proper married life, I can then find it really difficult. I'm guilty of all the things you read about that you shouldn't say. Reading between the lines of the welfare booklet, a "Don't" would be to say, "Don't you come home here and tell me what to do. Don't come back and start telling my children off. Don't tell me I can't do this or that." And I'm guilty of all of them. The "Dos" are "Do give him time to chill out and relax, do remember he has just been through one hell of an experience. Do remember that he normally wears the trousers."

'I read them and think, "Oops – I don't do that." I find it hard. Because hard as it is with them leaving, in the first month you get into a routine. You've got to cope on your own and make all the decisions. You're the only one there for the kids and to do that for six months is a long time, so to have somebody come in and start running things is hard. Mark's not bad – but, for instance, there are little things, like he'd go to put something on the telly – but I'll say, "Hang about now – I've been watching this on the other channel for the last few weeks. You haven't been here – so I'm watching this."'

It took about an hour and a half for Dai to sort out his kit and sign out – Julie waited for him in the Prince of Wales bar, but when they got back home it was like they had never been apart. 'It was a strange feeling,' she says. 'You see a change after a six-month tour. I was in a routine with the children, and he's got to fit back in. I think he thought when he came back he could lay down the law again – the rules in the house with the boys. But I didn't agree with it, I thought he needed a couple of days to settle back in, but he started straight away, I didn't think it was right. I think he thought he was still out there with his men – that was the problem. I had to sit him down and say, "Dai, I've been in a routine with the boys – you've got to fit back into OUR life now." It's a tough thing to say, I know, but otherwise the routine would have gone out of the window, and I had to keep things normal for our sons – just as I had had to do for six months on my own. We had a little chat and I don't think he realised what he was doing, but he tried his hardest to calm down a bit. It was like I had to remind him, "I'm your wife and these are your children – we're not soldiers."'

Tougher than adjusting to the minutiae of daily life is accepting the fact that your husband may have been changed by his tour – sometimes permanently. 'After the Iraq tour Mark was quiet for a while because he went through a lot and saw a lot of terrible things happen,' Simone remembers, 'but what was good was that he could talk about it. I encouraged him to try to talk to me about what he went through – I knew that if he didn't talk about it, things could get a lot worse for him. I'd come straight out and ask him, "Tell me what happened when so-and-so died. How did it happen?" He would answer me freely. We were lucky, a mate he was in Basra Palace with lives just round the corner, they shared a lot of the same experiences and I am friends with the wife. We would go round there for a cuppa, and they would talk about it endlessly because it was an experience they'll never have again, and talking to one another I think helped them while us wives could support one another – supporting our husbands.

'When he talked about when one lad died (not 2 Royal Welsh) it was horrible. Mark saw that boy being blown to bits. They were picking up parts of his body from all over the road and that poor boy couldn't be brought home to be buried for weeks and weeks because they couldn't put his body together. And Mark actually looked behind from his Warrior and saw this. You can't begin to comprehend. I kept trying to think, "How can that be?" But they're soldiers, they've got the right temperament and they just carry on – they've got to. Mark went over a roadside bomb himself – and I thought, "He must have been petrified," and every night he went out on patrol he admitted that he got that feeling in his stomach, "Will I be coming back from this patrol?" because it was so bad out there.'

Amanda agrees that many wives worry their husbands will be changed by a tour. 'That is what's scary,' she says. 'You want them back, but you don't know if you're going to get back the same man who went out. I did say that to Lee before he went, "I want you to come back, don't let it change you." It's so hard to see that change in someone you love. Op TELEC 3 (an even earlier Iraq tour) was the worst change, and it was for a lot of the men. That was in about 2003–4, our battalion had gone out as a whole and I don't know what sparked the chain of events, but a lot of wives, when the men came back, noticed a massive difference in their husbands. One of my closest friends, who lived next door to me at the time, knocked on my door, screaming to be let in. Her husband was probably the most placid man I'd ever met in my life, but her front door was covered in blood because he'd literally smashed out the back window of her car, where all the wire is for the heater – he'd just slashed his hands to bits and she'd never seen him like that before; he wasn't trying to hurt her, he was just filled with rage. Lee has never talked to me with anger, a big giant – he never gets angry, he's a pussycat. But at that time he was angrier than I'd ever seen him before.'

Despite the spectre of war that is inevitably brought home by a returning soldier, normal life must be lived and after around three days, just as it was when the men left, all the Daffodil Girls tell me they then feel it is time to 'get on with it'. 'When Mark's been back about three days, I find myself thinking, "That's it, you're back,"' Simone tells me with a smile. 'Get rid of the mess. It's about time now.' Kaz agrees, 'It's such a feeling when you have them back, it's lovely. You can't do enough for them – you spoil them – then by the Monday you think, "You've had your three days of being spoilt, now get out of your dressing gown and get on with it." But it is an amazing feeling to have them home.'

Amanda tells me, 'You romanticise them and you as a couple more when they're away. When they come back I would like to say it's everything you've thought and dreamt of – but it's not, it's totally different – the reality kicks in. You treat them like kings for about three days, by my reckoning. Then the fact that the boots have been left in the hallway and the bag is still waiting to be unpacked and you're tripping over it all starts to get on your nerves. You have your little gripes because you've lived apart for such a long time. You have to ease yourself back into a routine – it's not something that happens straight away.'

Ed and I – a relatively new couple – didn't have to slot back into married life when he came back from Iraq. But even as boyfriend and girlfriend, living separately, the period of adjustment was noticeable. I had, as Amanda said, romanticised while he was away, with a montage that wouldn't have been out of place in any rom-com – of candlelit meals, moonlit strolls, meaningful conversations and mini breaks – rolling through my head. But in reality I had work while he mooched around my London flat, bored. I wanted to talk for hours – he was so used to male company that he had pretty much lost the art of small talk and at night we struggled to sleep in the same bed.

After months camping in the desert Ed slept (and to this day – God help me – still does) on his back, hands behind his head, elbows sticking out and, inexplicably, his knees upright, creating a mini tent with the duvet. Inevitably, when sleeping like this, his knees will drop to one side, often hitting me in the side, or I get an elbow in the face if one of us rolls over and, of course, lying on his back, the predictable rumble of a snore will begin. Now, as a wife, I give him a shove and get him to roll over, moving his arms and knees out of my way, but back then, while he slept peacefully, I would lie there shimmering with frustration, knowing in a few hours I would go to work while he would get to stay in bed. To this day, and after five years together, despite buying the biggest bed that would fit in our bedroom, we still struggle to sleep in the same bed together; the months of separation mean we really still both sleep better when sleeping alone.

I am pleased to learn that it not just us – most of the Daffodil Girls tell me that this is normal, and reassure me that it is nothing that a long marriage won't cure. 'When Mark away I spread myself out,' Simone says. 'It is difficult when he's back in my bed and we have to get used to sleeping next to one another again. I do like having him to *cwtch* though.' Dereynn admits, 'It's strange having him back physically – your body has got to adjust to having someone else there, an extra pair of hands to help, someone else at the table, sat on the sofa, in your bed. Dad's here now, not just mum.'

After Craig's death, Donna decided not to return to her hometown of Catterick, choosing instead to live in the village in which Craig grew up. 'We were staying with Craig's mum and Bradley had started in the local school – I wanted to give him some normality,' she says. In October Donna was able to buy, with the compensation money paid to her as a widow by the MOD, a small terraced house near the school. Opposite a small park, the house has stunning views of the mountains opposite. She had it decorated, then moved in November. 'It's a lovely place,' she says. 'The view is the main reason I bought it and it's quiet and a nice area for Bradley.'

Three years on from Craig's death and Donna has gone back to university to do a health and social care degree. She wants to go into nursing and perhaps become a midwife. Talking to her, I was struck by how incredibly brave she is – picking herself up after the unimaginable and creating a life for her and her son. 'In the beginning I wouldn't have bothered to get out of bed,' she tells me, 'but I thought I've got a child here and he's done nothing wrong and he still needs to be looked after. He needs me and needs emotional support and if it wasn't for that, I don't know where I'd be now. I don't think I'd have been as strong as I have been and I don't think my future would be as clear as it is. When Craig died, our whole life crumbled, everything changed – the only thing that stayed the same was me and Bradley being together.'

In the first year after his death, Craig's family raised money for Help for Heroes, aware that Craig could have so easily been one of the wounded the charity supports. Now they raise funds for local projects – local rugby teams and the things he would have liked to have helped and been involved in as a child and older. 'Most important is keeping his memory alive,' Donna says, 'as long as we do that, nobody is going to forget him. Not that he was a character you would easily forget.

'We have done various things – there's a little park opposite my house and we've got a memorial bench in it with a plaque on – his friends raised the money for that. As you drive up, on the mountain, there's a flag overlooking the village. Craig's mum physically planted that, but it was my idea – we put that there and whoever sees it knows it's for Craig. When I was staying with Craig's mum, I was the only smoker, so being in the garden is where I'd do my thinking, looking up at the mountain. I said that on his first anniversary that I was going to walk up the mountain and plant a flag there – but it escalated and it's now a huge flag, cemented in, and there's a plaque and a bench to go in. The amount of people that go up there just to have a look at the flag is unbelievable. Every day I see at least one person walking up there. We're incredibly proud of him and we hope we're making him proud by keeping his memory alive

'You see pity on everybody's face – and although it's nice that they sympathise with you, it's not something you want to see. I don't tell a lot of people because I don't want to see the pity. I used to wear a pendant with a photo of us on and people would say it was lovely – but seeing my wedding dress in it they'd ask, "Oh, you've been married, have you?" and when I told them I could tell they did't know what to say. I want to tell people about him, but I don't want my whole life to revolve around me being his widow.

'Even now I wouldn't say I'm coming to terms with it – that it's properly hit me. I'm not sure that I've grieved as such. My plan all along was to be on autopilot and keep busy, and it still is. I can think and talk about it a lot more than I could before and Bradley is at school and quite happy – so it's all good. He does remember his dad – he comes out with things like, "Daddy used to do that", or, '"I used to go swimming with daddy, didn't I?" He brings him into the conversation and we talk about him a lot. If he says something Craig would say or do, I say, "Daddy would do that," and we have Craig's picture everywhere.

'I think about him all the time – in everything I do. I wonder, "What would Craig do? What would he say?" I think about the life we would have had and where we would have been now, what we would have been doing – would we have had more children? I suppose as well as grieving for my husband, I am grieving for the life we should have lived together.'

It was a day everyone had been looking forward to for months – since even before the tour began. Even though the men had all been home for at least a few days now, this was the day that really meant it was all over – the homecoming medals parade in Cardiff. The men were due to march from Cardiff Castle to the Millennium Stadium for a ceremony to welcome them home, to present medals to those for whom this had been a first tour and to remember those men who had not come home.

The day of the Iraq homecoming parade began early for the Daffodil Girls. The alarm clock rang when it was still dark but Amanda leapt of bed, shivering in the cold. She turned on the shower to warm up before waking Megan, then Bethan. Her outfit was already laid out on the chair in her room; a long skirt with thick tights, knee-high boots and a warm but pretty jumper – her coat would mostly cover it up, but Amanda hoped she'd look smart as well as keep warm. They drove into camp, the weak December sun beginning to appear, turning dark shadows into lighter shades of grey. Most of the wives who lived on the patch were there, accompanied by children old and young; it was blisteringly cold but no one cared. They clambered on to the waiting coaches, chattering with excitement, thick winter coats pulled tightly over smart suits and dresses. Amanda, with her girls, grabbed seats near the front and friend Simone sat down across the aisle with her sons.

There a fleet of fifty-two-seater coaches going from Tidworth and Amanda and her girls were in the first. There was a fantastic atmosphere onboard, everyone buzzing with excitement and desperate to get to Cardiff. The men had left even earlier to prepare so only families were in the convoy from camp. They hit a traffic jam just outside of Marlborough; there had been an accident, and Amanda started to worry that they were going to be late and miss the start of the parade. Finally, after more than an hour, they were through the jam and the buses arrived in Cardiff only fifteen minutes later than expected, still with enough time to get a good spot from which to watch the parade.

It was busy but Lee's parents and Amanda's mum and dad were, as arranged, at the coach drop-off point – they had travelled from their homes in Wales, so had not been on the coach from Tidworth. Amanda was surprised to also see Lee's Aunt Diana waiting with the parents and immediately started worrying – other than the tickets for herself and the girls she had only been given four tickets, one for each of their parents, for the ceremony taking place after the march and she was concerned about not being able to get a seat for Diana. But there was no time to try and sort it out then; the streets had been closed for the parade and the families and friends of the returning men, and the people of Wales, had turned out in force – the city was packed. Amanda grabbed her girls and pushed her way to the barrier by the entrance to Cardiff Castle where the parade was beginning.

It wasn't long before they heard the rumble of a tank starting and the band begin to play *Men of Harlech*. First came a Warrior – the vehicle that the men had used in Iraq, the Welsh flag aloft, then came the band of the Prince of Wales's Division, just before the returning soldiers, marching three abreast in their desert combats. Amanda heard Lee's voice, shouting in his booming sergeant major's voice, 'Left, Right, Left, Right'. Then he was there – wearing his khaki service uniform he stood out from the rest, his pace stick (a wooden stick with a brass end which opens up and is used to measure a soldier's marching pace) clutched under his arm. Amanda could see his chest was puffed up in pride – it was the first time that both their sets of parents had seen him in this role, in uniform, commanding his men. He was soon past her and Amanda tried to move down the barrier alongside her husband but the men were too fast and it was too crowded. There were more people than she had expected, Welsh flags were being waved and cheers of 'Well done', 'Welcome home' and 'Good job' came from the throng.

When Amanda realised she wasn't going to be able to

keep up with the men she went back to the castle entrance to find the rest of the family and they made their way to the Millennium Stadium, the home of Welsh rugby, to find their seats for the medal-giving parade and memorial service. Amanda needn't have worried about a spare ticket for Lee's aunt. At Gate Number 2 where they entered, a member of the welfare team was able to give her a spare, although he warned that it wouldn't be with the rest of the family. The stadium is huge, seating more than 74,000 spectators, but for this event only a small section was being used – around three thousand seats on two tiers. There were allocated seats for family and friends, but members of the public were also invited to come and find a seat alongside the reserved ones.

Amanda decided to let Diana sit with the rest of her family and went off to find herself a seat – she was only about five rows up but there was no one else in the surrounding seats, Amanda mouthed at her mother that if they didn't fill up she would be back down to join them. She looked around at the wide expanse of the stadium – the roof was closed, but it was still absolutely freezing and with so few seats being used and no turf down, just the concrete floor, it felt rather empty, barren almost. Soon all the seats around her started to fill up but when Amanda realised who she was sitting with, her heart became heavy. It was the family of one of the young boys who had been killed, Ryan.

Ryan had been killed the month before Craig, aged just twenty-three, and Amanda knew the family from the funeral and from visiting the parents a few weeks later. She knew what an ordeal this was going to be for them. Ryan's mother had obviously been crying already and as soon as she was able, Amanda mouthed down to Lee's parents to tone it down – they tended to get a bit carried away at occasions like this and Amanda knew that the last thing the grieving parents would need to see were another set of parents whooping for joy just five rows in front.

When everyone was seated, the Warrior parked up on the concrete, the band began to play again, leading the men in. The crowd erupted, clapping and cheering – but all Amanda could do was bow her head as she heard Ryan's mother's heart-broken sobbing behind her. On a table covered with the Welsh flag were five tall church candles – one for each of the men that had not come home, three Royal Welsh soldiers and two Black Watch who had been attached to the battalion for the tour. Amanda remembers looking at them and the men lining up behind and thinking 'Why them? Why not these men?' But she knew there was no answer.

Somewhere else in the stadium, Donna was sitting with Craig's mum, his nan and Bampy and his little sister Beccy. Despite wearing trousers and a thick coat, she was already freezing. Even before the service began, Donna was finding the day one of the most emotional since she had been told her young husband had been killed. Harder in a way than the funeral because, like Amanda, she couldn't help but look at the faces of the men standing on the concrete below and ask why her husband wasn't there with them. She remembers wanting Craig to be a part of it, to hear the cheers of the crowd. 'I was jealous,' she explains. 'These families were going to have something that I was never going to have – their soldier come home to them.'

It was a lovely service – Lieutenant General Sir Freddie Viggers, adjutant general for the whole of the army, took the lectern as guest of honour, standing in for General Sir Richard Dannett, then Head, who had been unable to attend due to illness. General Viggers thanked the returning soldiers for all they had done, then was followed by the commanding officer, who spoke of his pride in the men but also, appropriately, paid tribute to the families present saying, 'Thank you for your support because without it, I don't think we could do what we do.'

At different points of the service a eulogy was read for each of the fallen soldiers and a few verses recited. When Ryan's was read, Amanda reached over to pat the hand of the boy sitting next to her, his brother. The seventeen-year-old was crying silently, tears dripping off his nose, as the commanding officer praised his sibling. Amanda couldn't bear to turn to see how Ryan's mum was coping.

The medal parade for those men for whom this tour of Iraq had been their first took place – around a third of the men present stepped forward to receive a medal while their families clapped and cheered with pride. This had been the third tour of Iraq completed by the battalion in the past four years, so most of the men already wore the medal with its distinctive yellow ribbon (to represent the sand of the desert). Lee had his, but Amanda still clapped like mad as each lad received his. It was icy in the stadium and Amanda remembers thinking how cold the men must be, standing to attention in immaculate lines.

Towards the end of the ceremony a soldier stepped forward, barking out the lines familiar from numerous war

memorials and Remembrance Day services; the fourth
stanza of the Laurence Binyon poem *For The Fallen*,

They shall grow not old, as we that are left grow old:
Age shall not weary them, nor the years condemn.
At the going down of the sun, and in the morning
We will remember them.

The haunting notes of *The Last Post* then filled the
stadium and Amanda felt her eyes prick with tears.
Everyone's head was bowed and stayed bowed for two
minutes of silence; not a sound was made until the *Reveille*
sounded and the same soldier recited the epitaph,

'When you go home, Tell them of us and say,
For their tomorrow, We gave our today'

and in a poignant, painful moment, the padre stepped
forward and blew out each of the candles. Behind her,
Amanda heard Ryan's mum's sobbing increase. 'I didn't like
that, the candles being blown out,' Amanda says, 'it seemed
cold almost, but I suppose they must have thought it was
symbolic.'

The families and friends were then invited down to join
the men. Amanda paused for a minute – watching children
run into father's arms, wives kiss husbands proudly. She
didn't need to rush and knew Lee wouldn't want to kiss or
cwtch while he was in uniform. Next to her Ryan's family
were preparing to leave, the younger brother, to whom she
had tried to offer silent comfort during the service, asked

which her husband was. 'I said "The one with the big stick,"' Amanda remembers with a grin, 'but I think he misheard me because he started giggling and I said, "I did say *stick* you know," and he laughed. It was a light moment after a gruelling time for him, and their whole family.'

Amanda had enjoyed the day – seeing the soldiers that her husband Lee was so proud of, boys whom he said had become men in the six months they had been away, march on and receive recognition from the public in front of their loved ones, for what they had done. But always in the back of her mind were the families of the three 2 R Welsh and two Black Watch boys who didn't come back. As she travelled home, she stared sightlessly out at the wintry landscape and thought how easily a quirk of fate, or luck, or act of God, however you wanted to put it, could have made things so different. It could have been Donna, and the other bereaved mothers and girlfriends, who today had watched proudly while their boys marched through the streets of Cardiff . . . while Amanda's husband could have been the one who did not come home, represented only by a candle.

EPILOGUE

They hugged for ages – neither wanted to let the other go. Lucy squirmed in between them and it was the small dog's struggle to get free that finally made Ben and Kirsty pull away from one another. Ben was dressed in his MTP (multi-terrain pattern) uniform, holding his body armour, helmet and a bag. He put these on the kitchen floor, along with Lucy and stood back to look properly at his wife. Kirsty was wearing black leggings and ballet slippers, topped with a black-and-white striped tunic with large black corsage on the chest. The top showed off her bump perfectly which, with only five days to go until her due date, was easily twice as big as when Ben had left but he was still surprised, as he told his wife, as he thought it would be bigger.

The couple had, they hoped, timed things perfectly – Ben's R&R started five days before the baby was due, giving them some time together for just the two of them but still allowing for around a week once the baby came, so that Ben could see his child before he had to return to the front line. Of course there was a risk that the baby would come early or late, but the couple were optimistic that everything would go according to plan.

Kirsty went upstairs and ran Ben a bath, the first he'd had since he'd left for Afghanistan, and sat in the bathroom chatting to him while he lay in it. She didn't want to let him out of her sight for even a minute and had so many questions that she couldn't stop talking – Kirsty was relieved that her husband seemed to be the same as ever and upbeat, despite his months on the front line. The next few days were busy – they had lots to sort out before the baby came, jobs that Kirsty had been waiting to have her husband home before tackling – they put the finishing touches to the nursery, hung some pictures, sorted out their TV licence.

In the weeks before Ben came home, and after she had gone on maternity leave from Help for Heroes, Kirsty really hadn't felt up to doing much. She didn't like going for dog walks or to the supermarket on her own, feeling a bit too pregnant and worried she wouldn't be able to cope should something happen, so she had become, in her own words, a bit of a hermit. But now Ben was back she was relaxed about going out and about and, not wanting to leave his side, was happy popping to shops with him or taking Lucy down to the polo pitches for a run around. With Ben's arm to hold on too, she felt perfectly safe – she knew now he was back they were in it together, and she wouldn't have to cope on her own.

It was only after the due date had been and gone and there were only five days until Ben was due to return to

Helmand that they started to get worried. They tried all the old wives' tales: Kirsty ate a curry as hot as she could stand, they went on long walks, Ben went to Tesco to buy a fresh pineapple and she sat in front of the television perched on top of a balance ball, but nothing was happening.

Two days before Ben was actually due to return to Afghanistan, he had a phone call warning him that his flight had been brought forward by a day. The couple started to panic. It was a Sunday, so they were unable to call anyone in the welfare team, but on the Monday they spoke to Mo who said he would immediately send Ben's officer commanding out in Afghanistan an email. Mo requested that Ben's paternity leave begin on the day he was due back in Afghanistan to ensure, hopefully, that he would still be at home for the baby's birth. Originally the couple were going to have all of Ben's two weeks' paternity leave at the end of his tour because, unless there are extenuating circumstances, soldiers are not allowed to take this time during a tour. The couple had an anxious wait for the response and it wasn't until mid-afternoon that Mo called to let them know that it was OK – Ben had the extension. Thankfully, the OC agreed with Mo that Ben being there for the birth of his child was a priority. Now all they could do was wait.

By this point, all Kirsty wanted was for him to be there for the birth – anything else would be a bonus. A week later and nothing had happened and, finally, the midwife agreed that perhaps they should induce the labour – but only (as is the norm) when it was two weeks over the due date – the day before Ben was now meant to be flying back. The padre had reassured the couple that Ben would not be sent back while

Kirsty was still in hospital, but nothing was certain. 'We just decided that we weren't even going to think about when the flight would be,' Kirsty remembers. 'Instead, we just wanted to concentrate on the baby, and if he had to be whisked away the same night so be it, at least he would meet his baby first.'

Sunday morning, the alarm went off at 6.30: the couple needed to be at the hospital at eight and they wanted time in the morning to make sure they had everything packed and sorted. Kirsty again wore her black-and-white tunic, thinking it would be comfortable for as long as it took for the baby to come. The night before she had showered, washed and styled her hair to save time in the morning. Kirsty felt nervous and strangely sad to be leaving their dog. Lucy had been such a comfort while Ben had been away and they had spent so much time with her over the last few weeks while they waited for the baby to come that it felt odd to be leaving her alone until neighbours would collect her later that day. 'It seemed very real then,' Kirsty tells me. 'We were going in and knew we'd be coming back with a baby.'

Once at the hospital they parked and walked to the labour ward, Kirsty clutching Ben's hand tightly. She hadn't taken the midwife up on her offer of a tour of the hospital, so it was the first time she had seen it. At the ward they buzzed to be let in, and Kirsty was taken to a bed where she was going to be monitored. They needed to check the baby was happy before any final decision could be made. Once they were satisfied, the staff explained to the couple what would happen and warned that it might take two or three attempts to induce the delivery.

'We were panicking again at this stage,' Kirsty remembers, 'thinking that it might not happen for two or three days, so we were back to worrying that Ben might still have to get his Tuesday morning flight. The padre had said on the phone to Ben – "Don't worry – you'll be there for when the baby arrives. Keep us posted and we'll make sure you're around while Kirsty is in hospital – and we'll sort out another flight for you." So it did look as if that Tuesday morning flight was going to be a no-go. Everyone seemed to be doing their best to help us and we knew we had to trust the padre and the welfare team – and bless them, they were brilliant.'

The next few hours dragged endlessly. After the initial induction still nothing happened and the couple spent the time wandering around the hospital, stopping for cafe breaks and exploring the grounds, ringing both sets of parents a couple of times, to keep them in the loop. Every hour Kirsty would return to her bed so they could check that baby (and mum-to-be) was OK. It was afternoon by the time she started getting contractions – they began like quite mild period pains, quite low down, and coming every thirty seconds. But Kirsty was told these were artificial contractions brought on by the hormones which had been used – so the couple weren't moved to a labour suite. Kirsty was told to have a hot bath, and left to it. Ben went into the bathroom with his wife and they chatted while she gingerly lowered herself into the scalding-hot water. The pain was getting quite bad at this point but lying in the bath eased it and the couple talked happily – pleased that at last things were finally happening.

At 11 pm the midwife decided that Kirsty was in established labour and she was moved to a birthing suite. 'It was starting to get really painful,' she recalls, 'but I think I was quite polite about it – I didn't shout or scream. They offered me gas and air and said that I should have had it before. They said it would dull the pain – and it did. I started sucking on that and I didn't want to let go. Ben said he was quite shocked – or rather unnerved – watching me on the gas and air, apparently I became quite scary – intense. The anaesthetist came in and explained some stuff to me, and I was gazing at her and half taking it in. I said to Ben, as a joke, when she walked out of the room, "What did the big blue elephant say?" He believed me for a minute, then realised I was joking, but it made him laugh.'

The contractions were relentless and even with the gas and air there was no real respite from the pain for Kirsty. The couple had agreed that she should go for all the pain control she wanted and, as the pain got worse in the early hours of the morning, she decided to ask for an epidural. 'I was suddenly very anxious that the midwives were going to try to bypass offering me an epidural,' she tells me. 'I remember saying to Ben, "I think they're going to try to talk me out of it. Please don't let them . . . can you make sure I get an epidural, please?" After I asked about three times the midwife went and got the anaesthetist. I was so glad I did, because then I was able to get some sleep.'

It was six in the morning when Kirsty woke up – the midwife came to see her and after doing a routine check realised that the baby was about to arrive. 'I must have had a few hours' sleep,' Kirsty recalls. 'No one had examined me since I'd had the epidural – they'd just left me to it, because the monitor didn't show very strong contractions, but I think it must have just missed where they were. In the morning, when my midwife came to examine me, the head was there, crowning. I'd obviously been contracting in my sleep, in a big way, and she said, "We need to get this baby out."'

Ben was asleep in the chair next to Kirsty's bed but quickly woke up when Kirsty called out to him. The midwife started rushing about to get help and told Kirsty to push – even though she was numb and a little dazed Kirsty pushed down just twice and the baby was born, a little girl, and the midwife lifted her up and placed her on Kirsty's chest. She had planned for the first contact with her baby to be skin to skin but things had happened so quickly that she was still wearing her pyjama top. 'I don't think anyone was that prepared,' Kirsty says with a smile. 'The midwife just popped her on my front and there she was, looking a bit startled. It felt amazing – she looked perfect, not squished like some newborns do; Ben said she looked just like a little doll.'

Ben sat on the bed, putting his arm round his wife while they both stared down at their daughter in wonderment. They had already decided on names for a boy or a girl and knew as soon as they looked at her that the one they had chosen was perfect for their daughter – Annabel. The midwife took Annabel and gently swaddled her before handing her to Ben. He cradled his newborn tenderly and she curled her tiny fingers around his index finger – 'It was amazing,' Kirsty says with grin. 'I knew he'd be a natural dad, and he was – instantly, we were both instantly in love. I just couldn't believe she was here with us at last – it wasn't scary – I'm never afraid of anything when Ben's there, we're always been a team like that. But now we are a family.'

ACKNOWLEDGEMENTS

I am indebted to many people without whom it would have been impossible to write this book. The first, and biggest, thank you must go to the Daffodil Girls themselves for letting me into their homes and their lives: Amanda, Clare, Danielle, Dereynn, Donna, Elaine, Julie, Kaz, Kirsty, Louise, Mandy, Megan, Rhiannon, Sarah, Sian and Simone; I cannot thank you all enough for making the dream of this book a reality. Your stories (including those which, for various reasons, are not featured in the book) are so inspiring. Thank you for sharing them with me. Special thanks must go to Amanda who enabled all of this to happen; without her, the book could not have been written.

At 2 Royal Welsh, particular thanks must go to Major Richard Arden for his enthusiasm for the project from day one, Captain Justin Moynihan for his time and warm welcome at the welfare office and Lieutenant Colonel Didi

Wheeler, commanding officer of 2 Royal Welsh – thank you for saying yes.

Thanks also to Major Bob Hobbs and Sonja Hall at the MOD, for their hard work getting the relevant permissions needed for this book to happen, and for agreeing that this was a story that should be told.

The patch wives, from my husband's regiment and others, with whom dinner parties, glasses of wine, dog walks and cups of tea have not only helped me through the endless days of writing, but also infinitely enhanced my life, in particular Alana – whose friendship really has made Tidworth feel like home.

Thanks should go to Alex Christofi and the rest of the team at Conville & Walsh for all their efforts. The talented staff at Virgin Books have been amazing: Caroline Newbury in publicity, Louise Jones and Victoria Fiander in marketing, Phil Spencer in production and the sales team – their behind-the-scenes hard work is so appreciated. In particular I'd like to thank Yvonne Jacob, who has put up with endless panicked or over-excited phone calls, Louisa Joyner, who made the serendipitous phone call to Help for Heroes which started this whole thing, and Ed Faulkner for overseeing the book in Louisa's absence. Vicky Thomas, whose flawless and fast transcribing skills were invaluable and whose lovely emails were a huge encouragement in the early days of writing, and Bernice Davison, my copy editor, for meeting a very tight deadline with expert professionalism; and the fantastic proofreader Jo O'Neill deserve thanks, as does Sian James at the *Mail on Sunday* for giving me a taste for war reporting by sending me to Iraq and Afghanistan and for being a wonderful boss and friend. Help for Heroes deserves a thanks, too, for giving me a sabbatical to write this book and welcoming me back at the end of it. In particular, I'd like to thank Bryn and Emma Parry, the inspirational co-founders, and my colleagues and friends Rosie Trousdell and Jess Baker for their help with promoting the book, giving me essential social media lessons and for keeping H4H team PR running smoothly in my absence.

Thanks of course go to mum and dad for so many reasons and my wonderful in-laws, especially Sarah, who is the ultimate army wife and has taught me much.

Tom Bromley, my talented editor, has talked me down from many a ledge and guided me expertly along the rollercoaster ride that is every writer's first book. His gentle criticism and constant encouragement were invaluable – the Daffodil Girls would not be the book it is were it not for his expert direction. He has my heartfelt thanks.

I would not have been able to undertake this project, nor would I have completed it, without the unfailing support from my husband Ed – he has endured my frequent ups and downs with stoic patience, encouraged me and buoyed me up every step of the way. Understanding, loving and wise Ed – you are both my inspiration and my motivation. Really this book is a 262-page love letter to you.